WALKING IN CORNWALL

The Cheesewring towering above the quarry

WALKING IN CORNWALL

by

JOHN EARLE

CICERONE PRESS
MILNTHORPE, CUMBRIA

19. Mylor Bridge. Restronguet Passage 94
20. Manaccan. St. Anthony-in-Meneage. Dennis Head. ....
    Helford. Frenchman's Creek 96
21. Gweek. Pollard Farm. Boskenwyn Downs.
    Tolvan Cross 102
22. Lizard Point. Kynance Cove. Lizard Downs. Grade ....
    Church. Cadgwith 105
23. Redruth. Gwennap Pit. Carn Marth 111
24. Carnkie. Carn Brea 114
25. Chapel Porth. Carn Gowla. St. Agnes Beacon 117
26. Nancledra. Guval Downs. Castle-an-Dinas 120
27. Zennor. River Cove. Wicca Pool. Zennor Head 123
28. Men-an-Tol. Nine Maidens. Ding Dong.
    Lanyon Quoit 129
29. Chun Castle. Bosullow Village 134
30. Lamorna. Tater-du Lighthouse. The Merry Maidens.
    The Pipers 136
31. Treen. Logan Rock. Minack Theatre. Porthgwarra. ....
    Porthcurno 142

Long Walks 148
32. The Saints' Way Part 1: Padstow to Withiel 149
33. The Saints' Way Part 2: Withiel to Helman Tor 153
34. The Saints' Way Part 3: Helman Tor to Milltown 155
35. The Saints' Way Part 4: Milltown to Fowey 157
36. St. Michael's Way: Lelant to St. Michael's Mount 158
37. The Tinners' Way: St. Just to St. Ives 163
38. The Camel Trail: 1. Padstow to Bodmin. 2. Padstow to
    Poley's Bridge 170

Appendices
    Glossary of Cornish Place-names 172
    Useful Addresses and Telephone Numbers 173
    Bibliography 174

INTRODUCTION

I used to feel that Cornwall really only started beyond Penzance in what they call Penwith and ended with the towering granite cliffs of Land's End. It was the area that I knew really well from my childhood days, for my aunt, Kay Walker, was an artist in the Newlyn School in the early days of this century and we used to stay with her before the war. She lived in a glorious house called Myrtle, with Adams fireplaces and doors, high above Newlyn harbour. I still remember the two-day journey to Cornwall from Kent, where I lived, especially in the summer just before war was declared, with workmen painting white dots and lines on the roads in anticipation of the blackout.

When I came to live in Devon, just after the war, I was able to get to know much more of the rest of Cornwall and realized just how wrong I had been with my childhood assumptions and what a marvellous county the other parts of it are. This love of Cornwall grew over the years as I began to explore many of the corners I had not visited before, making films for television, and it was with delight that I began to undertake the research for this book. It gave me a chance to visit again the haunts of my youth and discover many more beautiful corners, though I still find that final granite thrust beyond Penzance the most exciting!

In my other two Cicerone guidebooks, *Walking on Dartmoor* and *Exmoor and the Quantocks*, most of the walks are on high moorland but in Cornwall, other than Bodmin Moor and the moors of Penwith, I found myself wandering into the depths of the beautiful Cornish miniature countryside and along the towering cliffs, over estuaries and across coves; a mass of delightful contrasts that make up this fascinating county of Cornwall.

You will be able to find wild open granite moorland, not so large as Dartmoor but with a lot of the same features, such as Bronze Age man's remains with stone rows, burial chambers, ancient field systems, all with that feeling of magic and mystery. Also on the moors are the old medieval farmsteads nestling below gaunt tors and nearby the quarries such as you find on Dartmoor.

Of course Cornwall is known for its spectacular coastline with hugh cliffs, sandy coves and small fishing villages with the protective arms of their little harbours, often tucked away in steep-sided valleys. In some of the villages you will find the stone walls of the old pilchard cellars where pilchards were cured and put into barrels for transporting to markets abroad and in this country.

You are never far from the smell and sound of the sea in Cornwall. There will be days when huge Atlantic rollers crash into the cliffs and rocks and you will have to struggle into the teeth of a gale with salt spray stinging your face and eyes. Then there will be tranquil, calm days with a glassy sea, copper-tinted by a hot summer sun and the air will be heavy and breathless; almost too warm for those tireless seabirds with their "wild white welter of winnowing wings" that swing and wheel around you with their evocative calls.

Deep lush country lanes will take you into the secret Cornish countryside with its abundance of wild flowers and wildlife.

All around the moors and along the coast are the gaunt chimneys of the engine houses of the once thriving mining industry, sadly no more, that was the lifeblood of Cornwall. The landscape has changed enormously since those days when the air must have been thick with sulphurous smoke not only from the great single-cylinder Cornish engines but all the other small industries that backed up the mining itself; blacksmiths making picks and shovels, coopers making barrels for the products of the region.

Around St. Austell there are what were once jokingly called the 'Cornish Alps, the conical tips from the china clay industry that still survives here. Nowadays, with care for the environment to the forefront, the china clay tips are landscaped and look more like Iron Age forts but I miss the 'Alps'.

But all is not beauty in Cornwall for it also has some of the most appalling holiday and tourist developments to be seen in Britain; sprawling holiday camps and caravan sites, huge car parks, beach cafes and other unsightly amenities. The shoreline itself often has a line of oil discharged at sea, plastic bottles, old nets and ropes and other rubbish, while the quality of the seawater itself is suspect in some areas. Thank goodness that a lot of the coastline is now protected by the splendid scheme of the National Trust, Enterprise Neptune.

You will find in this Guide, then, a wide variety of walks in a wide variety of landscapes that I am sure will delight and fascinate you.

THE GEOLOGY AND WILDLIFE OF CORNWALL

Natural history is determined by geology and therefore the soils of a region, and Cornwall is no exception. To this you must add the climate. Cornwall is almost an island, for the Tamar rises only a few miles from the north coast and flows south to the sea at Plymouth. There is a joke told that if the chains used by the Torpoint Ferry to cross the Tamar broke, Cornwall would float away! This peninsula juts out into the Atlantic with a relatively warm wet climate and fierce winds that roar in off the ocean. I propose to cover briefly the geology, wildlife and vegetation together in this one section of the book as they are so inextricably linked.

There are huge contrasts to be found in Cornwall and as you move around this is apparent immediately between the north and south of the county.

In the north you will find towering wild cliffs with very few estuaries and breaks in this savage coastline, with of course the exceptions such as the Camel and the huge sand-dunes of Perranporth and Hayle where the dunes are known as The Towans. These dunes have their own particular vegetation such as sea holly, burnet rose and sea rocket.

Again, except for the Camel, most of Cornwall's rivers flow to the south coast, often down deep wooded valleys, and the more gentle coastline is broken with wide deep estuaries. You will also find more salt-marshes on the south coast where sea spurrey and sea asters can be found.

The many rocky coves and sandy beaches that are a delight for children, wading about with buckets and spades and shrimping nets, are teeming with shoreline and marine wildlife and many different seaweeds. Mussels, whelks, limpets, barnacles, crabs, anemones and starfish are just a few of the creatures to be found on the rocks or in the pools.

Out at sea, just off the shore, you might be lucky to see basking sharks cruising round on hot calm June days or sometimes dolphins and small whales arrive to delight the tourists and even strand themselves on the beaches. Not so delightful are the jellyfish that float in from the oceans in warm weather. But of all the animals seen in the sea off Cornwall, it is the grey seal that evokes such memories, bobbing its head out of the water with its inquisitive limpid brown eyes watching you carefully in case you get too close. It is Britain's largest mammal and is found all round the Cornish coast but especially on the Isles of Scilly where they lie on the rocks having clambered out to rest, sometimes with their charming pups that are covered in long fine white hair at birth; they have a heart-rending, almost human wailing cry.

You are never more than 15 miles from the coast and the sea in Cornwall, often much closer, so it is the seabirds that are the most obvious, especially the gulls but also the neat little kittiwakes and fulmars. Razorbills and guillemots will be seen flying low and fast over the water and just a few puffins, now sadly depleted in numbers. Black shags and cormorants perch like funny old men with their wings stretched out to dry on the rocks offshore or will be seen diving for fish; it's always amusing to see if you can guess where they will surface again. The sands of the estuaries and salt-marshes are the homes for the waders such as sandpipers, godwits and the oyster-catchers.

Wild flowers grow in profusion along the coasts of Cornwall and you'll need a good reference book to recognise all the species you'll find, from buttercups to sheep's sorrel, bird's-foot trefoil to sea campion; it's a mass of colour and interest and what extraordinary names! Gorse, hawthorn and heather also thrive and many of the flowers and plants come into bloom at different times of the year so there always seems to be colour even on gloomy winter days when the sea mists roll in to the sound of baying foghorns.

Because of the underlying sedimentary rocks from the Devonian period such as shales, sandstones and the culm measures which formed the huge up-thrusted Armorican mountain system of two million years ago and the welling igneous instrusion of molten granite that forms the high moorland areas of Cornwall, the soil is more acid than most other parts of Britain and the vegetation and wildlife reflect this.

Ling, heather, and bilberry grow well on the moors such as Bodmin, but grazing by sheep has reduced the areas considerably.

In some of the boggier parts of the moors you'll find sphagnum moss, insect-eating sundews, bog asphodel, cotton grass and orchids, while by the tumbling streams are the ferns, yellow flags, marsh orchids and forget-me-nots.

Many of the birds associated with moorland areas are found in Cornwall such as lapwings, falling about the sky with their shrill peewit cries; there are also curlews and, sadly becoming rare, golden plovers. Both on the moors and above the towers of the rocky coast you'll see the moth-like wheeling buzzard with its shrill kitten cry, as well as kestrels and ravens. While, as on Dartmoor and Exmoor, the skylark pours out its bubbling song in "unpremeditated bliss". Meadow pipits and stonechats are also found on the Cornish moors.

The ubiquitous fox is a common sight slinking off at high speed, while badgers are seen both in the woods and on the edge of the moors where they build their setts in the granite boulders.

In May and June caterpillars and butterflies emerge including some uncommon species such as the green hairstreak, found where there are gorse and bilberries and the dark green fritillary.

Two of the walks will take you onto the Lizard, the most southerly point of mainland Britain jutting out just into the 40s latitudes. Geologically it is a most interesting area where the rocks are gabbro (found also in Skye), schists and serpentine which gives rise to the countless ashtrays, lighthouses and other tourist souvenirs made with this rock! As a result of these unusual rocks the flora is unique and attracts many botanists. They come to try to find rare clover and buttercups while Cornish heath, pygmy rush and orchids are of great interest.

Moving again inland into the secret Cornish countryside, some walks will take you into deep-cut lanes with ferns growing from the banks with masses of foxgloves, red campion, bluebells and many other hedgerow flowers that are one of the delights of Britain and especially Cornwall.

The dry-stone walls, one of the extraordinary features of the Cornish landscape, also have an environment of their own with lichens, rock spurrey and even the rare lanceolate spleenwort, while many small insects and creatures live in the crevices.

Finally you cannot miss the damp dense-wooded valleys, often with streams and rivers flowing through them, tumbling their way down to the sea. These are the ancient woods of Cornwall. Oaks, including the sessile oak which produces acorns without stalks, ash and holly grow here. Some of the woods are so old as to be mentioned in the Domesday Book. Sadly many have been felled or reduced in size for farming, mining and housing estates. In some areas regimented lines of conifers have been planted instead. It is vital that these deciduous woods are conserved, protected and allowed to flourish. They are the haunt of badgers, stoats, weasels, foxes, even a few red deer. The otter is returning to some Cornish rivers within these woods.

You will find wood anemones, bluebells and snowdrops thriving here along with mosses, ferns, fungi and the tree lungwort which is only found in areas where there is not a lot of pollution, which tells you something about the air in Cornwall.

I cannot leave a section about wildlife without mention of the red-billed Cornish chough. It is sadly extinct in this part of Britain, though it survives in Wales and Ireland. It still, of course, is used in the coat of arms of the county as it was once so common here that it became known as the 'Cornish' chough.

You will realize by now what a rich and varied area Cornwall is for all wildlife. There are over 60 Sites of Special Scientific Interest and the Lizard National Nature Reserve. The National Trust owns hundreds of miles of the coast. The Cornwall Trust for Nature Conservation has under it some 28 nature reserves which in all cover over 3000 acres. But in spite of all these worthy bodies this is a heritage that must be protected and conserved against the horrors that still go on such as felling woodlands, some types of farming, roads, building, industries, and over-use of some areas. You can probably name and will see more scandalous destruction of the rich Cornish landscape. Only by educated, careful and caring use by us all will it survive.

MAN IN CORNWALL

Smugglers, wreckers, tin and clay workers, farmers, fishermen, saints and rugby players. For many people this list probably sums up 'Man in Cornwall'. But it only scratches the surface of the long history of man here that stretches back even beyond 8000 BC.

The landmass of the whole of Britain was larger in this early period of history but as the climate warmed up, after the Ice Age, the level of the sea rose because of the melting ice and the estuaries and coastal lowlands were drowned. The arctic vegetation changed and in Cornwall there were coniferous and oak forests where roamed deer, wild pigs and ox. Nomadic Mesolithic man hunted these animals as well as gathering berries and nuts. To supplement their food they probably fished and hunted seals as well as collecting shellfish. All that remains of these early Cornishmen are a few flint implements.

After these hunters and gatherers we find man starting to farm the land from about 4000 BC. He cleared the woods to grow crops and started to change the landscape of Cornwall. There are many small plots, huge stone ramparts and both round and rectangular houses still to be seen. Neolithic man made stone axes and pottery which he traded; some of these early Cornish 'souvenirs' have been found in Essex and other parts of Britain. These were the people who, with immense toil and skill, made the great megalithic burial chambers, the quoits, we can still see today; some of the walks will visit these.

We come now to the Bronze Age from 2000 to 600 BC. Parts of Cornwall like Dartmoor are rich in remains from this prehistoric period. You will find their circular huts and field systems, many ceremonial stone rows and circles, burial mounds and menhirs. If you look at the maps you will see countless barrows or tumuli that were the huge cairns built over the cremated remains of ancient leaders and headmen.

Perhaps the moors near Land's End and Bodmin Moor are the best areas to see their hut circles and the lynchets, the terraced fields, where they would have broken the soil with primitive wooden ploughs for crops, for these men were farmers as well as stone row and ceremonial builders.

It is also in this period that the Cornish tin and copper industry started, for bronze is made from a mixture of these two minerals found around the igneous granite intrusions. They made weapons and jewellery in their small smelting furnaces, while they traded for gold to make armlets and other ornaments such as collars. Some lovely examples have been found and can be seen in museums.

But the Bronze Age gave way to Iron and we move into the period of the Celts from 600 BC until just after the birth of Christ. These were the people who constructed the hill-forts in Cornwall with huge ramparts and ditches. They were the strongholds of the tribal chiefs of this time. Around them but also defended were the smaller dwellings and farms often forming small villages set in fields that can still be seen surrounded by stone walls. Chysauster and Carn Euny are fine examples of these Iron Age villages with an open courtyard, small houses and a fogou, a narrow low covered passage that may have been used for storage or possibly some form of ritual.

The Romans arrived now in Britain and while they pushed as far west as Exeter (Isca Dumnoniorum) they did not really march further into Cornwall. They ruled the Celtic tribes of Cornwall, Devon and West Somerset, called the Dumnonii, from Isca and the furthest west they got was to build a fort at Nanstallon near Bodmin. Cornwall remained essentially Celtic and the only change that occurred was for the people to move off the uplands and develop new settlements on the lower areas; the pattern of these villages remains to this day.

From the 5th century onwards Celtic kings ruled Cornwall but the English, following the Romans, came as far west as the Tamar in the 8th century and by the 10th had taken over control of Cornwall. The last Cornish king Dumgarth was drowned in 875 and this was the end.

During the Celtic years the people lived in enclosed hamlets but as they moved away more from growing crops to keeping animals their villages were no longer enclosed and the houses changed from being round to rectangular, often surrounding a courtyard.

Living so close to the sea it is no wonder that many of the people were fishermen and traders going as far as the Mediterranean; traces of pottery from there have been found. But moving the other way from the Mediterranean and also from Wales we now have the arrival of Christianity in Cornwall bringing huge and important changes.

The 'Forth an Syns' or the Saint's Way is one of the walks that follows a route taken by the early saints from Wales, Ireland and Brittany across Cornwall between AD 400 and 700, the Dark Ages as we know this period of history.

There is a splendid adage that says that "Cornwall boasts more saints than were ever enthroned in heaven"! If you look at the maps of Cornwall almost every village seems to be named after one. St. Agnes, St. Austell, St. Buryan, St. Cleer, St. Day, St. Ives, St. Endellion, St. Just, the list goes on and on. There are extraordinary stories told about how some of them arrived in Cornwall. One on a mill-stone, another in a barrel, the saints from Brittany floated in on their stone altars and one even came over on an ivy leaf! St. Piran the patron saint of tinners was said to be something of a boozer!

However they arrived they set up 'cells' or churches to help convert the local people to Christianity and these were often built near the holy places of the ancient heathen religions such as springs, wells or the old standing stones. As you will discover their names live on in over 200 churches, many villages and towns and of course their annual feast days.

Without doubt these good men and women certainly had enormous influence and many of the Celtic kings and chieftains gave land where monasteries and colleges were built. The best known saint perhaps was St. Petroc who travelled widely in the West Country and even Brittany to found monasteries in Padstow and Bodmin. It was also at this time that the Celtic crosses that you will see were put up in churchyards and along the lanes.

As with the rest of Britain the Norman conquest was also to change life in Cornwall. The Normans arrived with their aristocracy and as in other parts of Britain built their fine castles in the county that still stand today: Launceston, Trematon, Restormel and Cardinham.

Life for the ordinary people revolved round single farms and small villages surrounded with strips of fields protected by low banks.

As we move into the 12th, 13th and 14th centuries, the medieval period, the beautiful Cornish churches were built and many fine houses with their chapels. Most of the small market towns were founded in this period of history and of course the fishing villages from which the inhabitants traded with Brittany, Spain, Ireland and Wales.

The French and the Spanish sent over raiding parties and as a

in from France with the contraband and the shore party who had to help land the goods, often heavy barrels or casks, and then get them up the steep and dangerous cliffs and away from the coast as quickly as possible before daylight. Those on the ship had to keep a close lookout for the revenue cutters that sailed the Cornish coast and the Preventive boats that worked closer inshore. Those on the shore, often teams of over 100 men, had to watch out for an ambush from the Preventive men on the land. It was a duel of wits. Fires of gorse were often lit to warn the boats coming in with the kegs of cognac (known as 'cousin Jacky'), bales of silk, tobacco, even dutiable manufactured glass, that the Preventive men were about and there are records of men being brought to trail for lighting such fires. Rewards were offered for information. But there is an old saying that goes "A Cornish jury will never convict a smuggler":

> *If you meet King George's men dressed in blue and red,*
> *You be careful what you say, and mindful what is said.*

For years smuggling continued and many true and extraordinary stories were told about the exploits. There were John and Harry Carter who worked in the area around St. Michael's Mount near Marazion. John called himself 'The King of Prussia' and indeed one of the secret coves where he operated is still known to this day as Prussia Cove. The names are endless and the places where they met and hid the contraband can still be seen. Many a house, even churches had secret chambers, tunnels and false floors. Jamaica Inn is just one inn where the smugglers met and hid their haul and themselves:

> *Five and twenty ponies trotting through the dark,*
> *Brandy for the Parson, baccy for the Clerk.*
> *Laces for a lady, letters for a spy.*
> *Them that asks no questions isn't told a lie.*
> *Watch the wall, my darling, while the Gentlemen go by!*

And what about the wreckers? Once again many fanciful tales are told but the stories of ships being lured onto the rocks by decoy lights are probably exaggerated. Beachcombing after a wreck however was probably yet another legitimate way of easing the hard lives that many of the Cornish lived in the 18th century and without doubt wholescale plundering took place sometimes, even when the crews were still on board. I fear that some were deliberately drowned or killed while trying to protect their cargoes. Parson Troutbeck of the Scilly Isles probably summed up the attitude to wrecks and wrecking when he said "We pray, O Lord, not that wrecks should occur, but that if they do, Thou wilt drive them into the Scilly Isles, for the benefit of the poor inhabitants"!

I cannot leave a section on the people of Cornwall without mention of the Cornish language. Dolly Pentreath, a fisherwoman from Mousehole who died in 1777, was said to be the last person to speak the Cornish language and nothing else. Recently there has been a renewed interest in Cornish and there are quite a number of evening classes to be found and it is taught in some schools. It is of course an old Celtic language with great links and similarities with Welsh and Breton as well as Scots, Irish and Manx. The Romans did not really push west into Cornwall and so this pocket of the Celtic language remained and indeed survived until the 18th century when closer links with England and the Anglican church brought about its decline. In the 14th and 15th centuries it was a rich and expressive language with much poetry and drama being written. Even now the old Celtic traditions and mysteries are celebrated with the annual Gorsedd of the Bards of Kernow where poems and other writings in Cornish are read and songs are sung by local choirs. Cornish wrestling and hurling are still practised, while on May Day the Padstow 'Obby 'Oss is led through the streets by the 'teazer' and in Helston on Flora Day you will see the ancient 'Hal-an-Tow' play. All these events have their roots in an ancient, mysterious Celtic past which is still strongly felt and forms a vital and intrinsic part of the lives of true Cornishmen. There is a deep-rooted nationalistic feeling and 'Home Rule for Kernow' is more than a pipe dream for some. The fervour, atmosphere and pride when Cornwall won the Rugby County Championships at Twickenham were something I shall never forget!

LEGENDS AND MYTHS
It is no wonder that such a Celtic country should have a host of legends, myths and folklore from giants, fairies and piskies to mermaids! I could fill several chapters with these tales. Perhaps the most fascinating and well known is King Arthur. Tintagel Castle

has always been associated with King Arthur and indeed there is evidence of a Celtic royal household but the remains there today are clearly Norman. However when Tennyson wrote "Dry clashed his harness in the icy caves and barren chasms, and all to left and right the bare cliff clanged about him as he based his feet on juts of slippery crag that rang sharp smitten with the dint of armed heels" he could well have had the dank forboding cliffs below Tintagel Castle in mind. One of the walks will take you there to see.

Castle-an-Dinas is another possible site for Arthur, as this Celtic hill-fort was indeed the home of the Cornish kings. The last and terrible battle of Arthur against his nephew Mordred is by tradition supposed to have taken place at Slaughterbridge on the River Camel near Camelford, while Dozmary Pool, only 6 miles away, is where Sir Bedivere went to return Excalibur to the "arm clothed in white samite...that gently drew him in the mere". And Boscastle with its narrow gulf of an entrance to the harbour could be from where Arthur was taken in his funeral barge to Avalon, "And on the mere the silence died away". Romantic and fascinating stuff!

And the legends and myths go on: Tristan and Iseult; The giant Bolster; Jan Tregeagle hunted by the devil on Bodmin Moor and then after his death carrying out his impossible tasks of moving sand to form Loe Bar and block the Camel or emptying Dozmary Pool with a limpet shell with a hole in it. Then there are the stories associated with saints such as Saint Piran and St. Petroc, not forgetting the piskies and the Mermaid of Padstow. I will come back to some of the legends during my descriptions of the walks, as they are so closely linked with parts of Cornwall. There are also many books that will help you find more.

CORNWALL TODAY

Cornwall, because it is small, is particularly vulnerable to modern pressures. The pressures from tourists and indeed walkers are enormous, though it is not just tourists who cause problems - I have mentioned some of the conflicting interests and the appalling developments that have been allowed.

Clearly as the horrors of urban life build up, more and more people will try to escape into the quiet and peace of the countryside - but do we all really want that? I sometimes doubt it when I see the crowded car parks and beaches, traffic jams in narrow lanes, lovely picnic sites with people sitting cheek by jowl, loud with blaring radios and ankle-deep in litter. By coming to Cornwall in such numbers we are destroying the very thing we are looking for. There has to be some control but mainly discipline, money, understanding and education to make sure that Cornwall retains its beauty and wildness.

To start protecting this heritage you could find no better advice than the **Country Code.**

1.   Guard against all risk of fire.
2.   Fasten all gates.
3.   Keep dogs under proper control.
4.   Keep to paths across farmland and then only if there is a right of way.
5.   Avoid damaging fences, hedges, walls and gates - particularly by climbing over them.
6.   Leave no litter - take it home.
7.   Safeguard water supplies.
8.   Protect wildlife, wild plants and trees. Do not pick flowers.
9.   Drive and walk carefully on narrow country roads. (It is important to know how to back up your car and be prepared to do so!) Park sensibly and carefully, not in front of gates or in narrow lanes or, for that matter, busy roads.
10.   Respect the life of the countryside and those who live there.
11.   Do not make unnecessary noise.

Access can also cause problems. It is no wonder that some Cornish farmers still regard the tourist as a scourge. I have seen people tramping across a fine crop of hay to have a picnic. All too often groups will climb over walls and fences to cut off a corner. I have watched dogs completely out of control chasing and yapping at sheep and cattle. I have heard farmers complaining of gates left open that allow their animals to wander onto roads or stray into fields where they should not go. We have all found empty tin cans and broken bottles left lying around; a terrible danger to livestock. Cigarette packets and butt ends, fish and chip papers, crisp and sweet packets and fried chicken cartons all litter popular areas and some of the beaches.

The public footpaths and bridle-paths are clearly marked on the maps you will be using. Many of them are also waymarked with posts and boards. Please stick to and respect the rights of way and do not stray off them. As a good general rule you can assume that all enclosed fields are private and that you should not enter them unless there is a marked right of way either on the map or by a sign.

The environment is not infinitely self-restoring. Damage is mostly the result of ignorance, thoughtlessness or carelessness. Man is part of this eco-system and his awareness of the problem and how to preserve and conserve it, and how to develop care and concern should not give rise to restriction but freedom with responsibility.

WHERE TO STAY

Cornwall is of course geared up for the tourist industry; an important economic factor for the county. During the peak holiday periods the whole area can become almost impossibly crowded and, in spite of vastly improved main roads there will be delays and traffic jams at some of the notorious black spots. There is a saying that goes "as the last car crosses the Tamar into Cornwall, the first one gets pushed off Land's End". The Cornish have a dialect word for tourists, 'emmets', which I gather means an ant! I leave you to work out why!

In spite of that slightly derogatory title the Cornish are, on the whole, a very welcoming people, though many of the hotels and guesthouses are run by people from 'up country' who came here on holiday, fell in love with the area and stayed to make their lives there. Birmingham and north country accents are the main ones heard in a lot of shops, cafes and bed and breakfasts.

Camping is possible as there are many sites scattered around the county. You can get a list of them from the Camping and Caravanning Club of Great Britain, 11 Grosvenor Place, London SW1W 0EY. The main tourist information centres will also help.

On some of the walks you may like to camp 'wild' but at all times, if you are not camping on a site, you must ask permission from the landowners who are mainly, of course, farmers. Most are friendly and will have no objections.

There are also quite a number of youth hostels.

Lastly of course there are hundreds of small bed and breakfast establishments and guesthouses from bungalows to large mansions and many farms. If you can get to Cornwall in the off-season there should be no need to book but during the school holidays it might be worth planning ahead, especially if you want to stay in one area and maybe do a number of the walks around that part of the countryside.

Cornwall is famous for its hotels, again ranging from the large and luxurious to the small and homely, and of course there are many first class restaurants, many specialising in seafood. The tourist information offices will help you find accommodation while some newsagents will have books and lists to help you find what you want.

MAPS AND COMPASS

At the moment the Ordnance Survey do not publish any 1:25,000 Outdoor Leisure Maps of Cornwall; I suppose it is too diverse an area. However you can get the 1:25,000 Pathfinder maps but of course you would need a large number to cover all of Cornwall. Perhaps you might like to buy some for the actual areas where the walks go as they are marvellous maps for details of walls and buildings, and the differences in terrain and heights are seen much more easily; a great help when navigating, especially on moorland in bad weather.

The most useful maps then and the ones which I have used for most of the time while writing this Guide are the Landranger Series of Great Britain based on a scale of 2cm to 1km (1:50,000) or about 1¼ inches to the mile. You will need five of them to cover all of Cornwall: numbers 190, 200, 201, 203, 204. I expect that you will be centred on one area and will only have to buy one or two to cover the walks in that area and some of the walks do not really need a map other than the ones provided in this book.

There will be occasions when sections of the walks on the moors of Cornwall will be so featureless, or you are in thick mist or walking at night, that you will not be able to navigate visually either by lining up features or walking towards known points identified both on the map and on the ground. It is then that you will have to rely on your compass by taking and using compass bearings.

Make sure that you buy a reliable, well-known make of compass. You will need a proper navigating compass as the small button compasses you can buy are of no use. They should have a clear plastic base like a protractor with a swivelling capsule to house the needle which should be luminous for night navigation.

An ability to use a map and compass is essential in wild country, but with this ability you should be able to find your way around the moors and certainly the lower walks in this book. You will need to know how to give and read six-figure map references. There are books that will help you listed at the end of this Guide if you have a problem here. Navigation is a complex, fascinating and satisfying subject and well worth following up. It may be just as well to have more than one person in your party who is competent with a map and compass!

One final bit of advice. I should get a good large waterproof map case or cover your map with a clear plastic self-adhesive sheet or maybe spray it with one of the waterproofing fluids that are available. Wet windy days in Cornwall, and there are quite a few of them, can quickly destroy a map!

CLOTHING

I do not intend to say much on this subject as most people who walk a lot will probably already have comfortable, warm and waterproof clothing and a small day rucksack. I suppose comfortable, warm and waterproof sums it all up; need I say more? But certainly for the high walks on Bodmin and the other moors your clothing must be good. I cannot emphasize enough the careful choice of boots and it is worth spending a lot of time in a reputable equipment shop talking to them about boots and trying on several different makes and styles.

USING THIS GUIDE

It has been difficult to know how to group the walks as there are no sensible boundaries to use. I have therefore started in the east and worked westwards. As the area of the whole of Cornwall is fairly small it means that you can base yourself either in the east, centrally or finally in the far west and find enough walks I hope within striking distance to keep you busy!

Because public transport is sadly limited in Cornwall I am assuming that most of you will be travelling by car. For this reason

I have tried to make the walks circular where possible except of course the long distance walks mentioned.

I have graded the walks firstly by length:

Long:	12kms or more
Medium:	4kms to 12kms
Short:	under 4kms

Secondly, I have classed the walks Hard, Moderate and Easy, depending on the difficulty of the terrain, the climbing involved and the map-reading and navigation skills needed. With the last however, on open moorland, it is wise to remember that what may be easy on a clear day will become tricky if the mists come down or if it is wet and windy, which it often is in Cornwall!

I shall assume that you will be able to find your way to the starting point of the walks by car from the six-figure map references, but I must admit that the maze of small lanes in parts of Cornwall can be confusing!

I give left and right as if looking in the correct direction of travel but I use the *true* left and right when talking about the banks of streams and rivers; in other words looking downstream.

I do not give the time I think the walks will take, as each of you will need to work it out for yourself depending on the age and fitness of your party and whether you want to wander gently, exploring and looking at things as you go, or put your head down and rush round as fast as you can go. I hope it will be the former!

Sometimes you will be passing places or objects to which I have referred in the early introductory sections so you may need to check back to the relevant pages but I shall hope to add more information wherever possible and indeed introduce new topics of interest.

With some of the walks it will be possible to shorten them by cutting off corners and leading back onto the route at another place. Even if I have not indicated this in the description of the route, by studying the map you will be able to make your own cuts, I am sure, if you wish.

Equally so you might well find that you can cut into the walk from a starting place of your own choice, different to the one that I have suggested, but please be careful where you park if you do this. I hope that you will use this Guide as a basis for walks that you can work out for yourselves, rather than following slavishly the exact routes that I have described. Obviously though I hope that you will follow some of my walks as they are all ones that I have enjoyed over the years or have found while writing this book.

I hope too that those of you who cannot walk or may not want to walk will also be able to use this Guide so that, with the aid of a map and what I have written, you will be able to come on some of the walks with me in your imagination and find out more about this beautiful and fascinating Celtic county of Cornwall.

All that remains now is for me to wish you safe, enjoyable and interesting walking.

New bridge over the River Tamar. (Walk 1)

The Walks

1. GUNNISLAKE. THE RIVER TAMAR. NEW BRIDGE. WOODS. CHAWLEIGH CLOSE.

Distance: Medium 3.5 miles / 5.6kms

Difficulty: Easy

Maps: Pathfinder 1340; Landranger 201

Start: Gunnislake station. Map Ref. 427711. Having said that public transport was lacking in Cornwall this walk proves the exception. You can catch the train from Plymouth to Gunnislake that follows BR's marvellous Tamar Valley Line. How long will it last, I wonder? There are also buses from Tavistock. If you come by car you can park at the station.

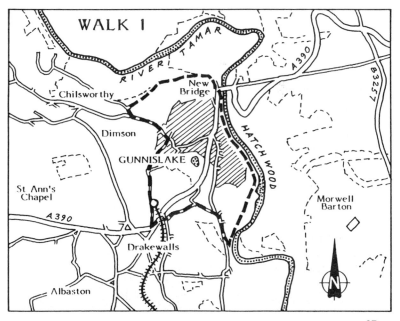

Gunnislake is the upper tidal limit of the Tamar. All around are the remains of the old tin and copper mines and these ores, as well as wolfram and arsenic, were taken from here down the river by vessels capable of taking 300 tons. Just down the river is Morwellham, another port for the ores, which is now an archaeological museum and well worth a visit. Devon Great Consols and Bedford United Mines are the two most famous in the area. The town itself has narrow streets of miners' cottages rising steeply up the hill from the river. There are shops and pubs in the village to provide for your needs.

There is a bit of road walking on this route but I wanted to have the first walk right on the Devon border and this was the only one I could find here. Set off along the station road to the A390.

A narrow gauge line was first built here in 1872 from Kelly Bray for the East Cornwall Mineral Railway to take ores to Calstock Quay. Early this century it was extended to Plymouth; the line we see today. There was another means of transport in the area too, for from 1800 until 1914 there were the beginnings of an extraordinary project called the Tamar Manure Navigation Canal which was part of an ambitious plan to build a canal from the Bristol Channel to the English Channel from Bude via Launceston to Gunnislake. It came to nothing but 600ft of it was built here and used until the First World War.

Turn left and go under the railway bridge and follow Well Park Road for some 100yds and then turn down towards the River Tamar. At the junction go to the right for about 300yds before forking left down the signposted footpath. When you reach the river turn north (left) and walk along the bank. You will pass old limekilns.

As I mentioned earlier quite large ships as well as smaller boats came up to here. The roads at the beginning of the last century and indeed well into this century were not good and using the River Tamar was the main means of transport in the area for limestone, coal and then of course the lime itself as well as the ores. To help navigation they built a canal in this area and you will see the weir. This marks the limit of the tides and, of course, the change from salt to fresh water. In medieval times fish traps were built at the weir and many fine Tamar salmon must have ended up in them.

In Devon, on the other side of the river, you will see Hatch Wood and towering out through the trees are the dramatic Morwell Rocks. There are some excellent, if loose, rock climbs here. It is a lovely walk along the riverside path with the Tamar beside you mostly tranquil but after heavy rain brown and sinister.

After a while you will reach the elegant New Bridge with its seven arches spanning the Tamar. *It was built in 1520 and it was then the lowest crossing point of the river and remained so until the building of the Tamar Bridge at Saltash in 1962. For many people this was their first way of entry into Cornwall and jokes are still made about needing a passport.*

There was a bloody battle here during the Civil War when the Royalists led by Sir Richard Grenville tried to prevent the Parliamentarians under Lord Essex taking the bridge. It was a fearful fight but eventually the Parliamentarians won the day, though not until 40 of them had been killed. This was nothing to the 200 Royalists who perished on that day.

Cross the road with New Bridge on your right and the old garage, which was once the site of a miners' hostel, on your left. Don't go through the gates to the right but walk on up the track into the woodland. When you reach a signpost fork left on the waymarked path and do not go up the steps also on the left. This will take you towards Hawkmoor Cottage. The track then follows a narrow steep path along a ridge through the woods.

The whole area here is a delightful ancient woodland with willows, oaks and hazels. The woods are also an old common and hidden in the trees are the remains of the Gunnislake Clitters Mine, yet another of the derelict mines in this area that produced tin and copper and the by-product arsenic. The ruins of old mines will be seen on very many of the walks in this book and it is appropriate that there should be one on the very first walk. It is amazing to think that this particular mine was working right up to the 1920s.

On the top of the ridge you will see a gap in the corner of the stone wall to your left. Go through it and follow the path until you reach the houses to your right and a signpost in the lane.

I'm afraid that it is road walking now back to the start. It's left and left again at the road junction until the T-junction where you swing right past a telephone box. Do not stray off either left or right along a road or a path. You will soon reach the A390 so it's downhill and left up Chawleigh Close back to the station and your car or the train back to Plymouth.

2. KINGSAND. CAWSAND. PENLEE POINT. RAME HEAD. WIGGLE

Distance: a. Medium 5 miles / 8kms
                b. Medium 7 miles / 11kms

Difficulty: Easy

Maps: Landranger 201; Pathfinder SX 45 / 55

Starts: There are in fact three starts, the choice is yours. The first is the large car park in Cawsand, Map Ref. SX 432503. Obviously this one is in a village where, coupled with Kingsand, are all the amenities you might need like shops, pubs and so on. The other two are car parks out in the countryside. One is on Rame Head beyond the little church with the spire in the village of Rame, SX 421488. The other is on the coastal road, SX 419504. However I shall describe the walk as if you are starting at Cawsand.

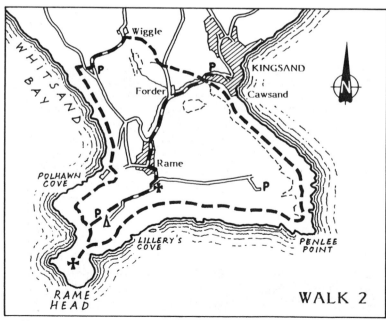

Both Kingsand and Cawsand are delightful unspoilt little fishing villages with steep twisting streets and a history that goes back to the Middle Ages. It is hard to know where one village stops and the other starts but locals say that the small stream that runs down to the sea here was the ancient border between Saxon England and Celtic Cornwall and marks the boundary. Indeed Kingsand was not part of Cornwall until 1844 and in Garrett Street you will find Boundary Cottage and the old marker on the wall next door shows where this extraordinary ancient boundary ran.

Today Brittany Ferries sail across to Roscoff from Plymouth but early in the last century it was the smugglers who made this journey, often landing at Kingsand and Cawsand with cognac and silks. In 1804 it is said that 17,000 casks of spirits were bootlegged year after year through the villages and probably into the many caves nearby, before ending up in the ready markets of nearby Plymouth.

Set off from the car park into Cawsand itself and then the little square. There is a lane to the left of the church which you can follow but there are also signs earlier marking the way to the Coastal Path by following Piers Lane. Whichever you take you will need to get onto the lower track of Earl's Drive to Penlee Point. *This is a*

Adelaide's Chapel

carriageway built by the Earls of Mount Edgcumbe in the early 18th and then into the 19th centuries. A lot of this walk is within the Mount Edgcumbe Country Park.

The drive runs through an avenue of fine trees which make it difficult to see the view off to the left except in winter of course. But you will have seen earlier, no doubt, the amazing breakwater, lying across the entrance to Plymouth Sound. Southerly gales used to build up huge seas in Plymouth Sound and many ships were lost, including ships from the Royal Navy, trying to get in and out of this natural harbour. As far back as 1788 discussions took place with a view to building a breakwater but nothing more happened. But by 1806, after still more wrecks, the famous Scottish engineer John Rennie was commissioned to draw plans for such a breakwater. Once again there were delays but at last, after many more ships and men were lost trying to get into Plymouth, work started in 1812. The labour of getting the huge foundation blocks into position was desperately difficult and it took until 1841 to finish the project with over 4^{1}/2 million tons of granite and limestone at a total cost of £1^{1}/2 million; a lot of money for those days. It is amazing that it took so long to get the breakwater built when, quite clearly, it was vital to the safety of both ships and their crews.

At the eastern end there used to be the Mariner's Cage. It was a huge round steel cage set on a pole high above the breakwater. In violent storms the sea actually breaks over the sea wall and any survivor from a shipwreck who had managed to get so far would have been swept off into the raging seas again. The idea was for the sailors to climb up into the cage and wait for the storm to subside and rescue to arrive. It was said to be able to hold as many as 16 men.

As the path swings south towards Penlee Point you will see on the hill up to your right a strange folly tower in ruins.

The track climbs now and near the coastguard station you will come across a grotto, another folly, called Adelaide's chapel, though of course it was never used as such. *It was built in 1827 by the Earl of Mount Edgcumbe in honour of Princess Adelaide, the wife of Prince William who was later to become King William IV. Apparently she used to stay at Mount Edgcumbe and enjoyed her visits to Penlee Point.*

Turn west now and follow the coastal footpath over the stile and on towards Rame Head. *The areas of steep hill and cliff below you to your left have fine names: Watch House Field; Middlebarton Brake and Homebarton Hill. This is a marvellous area for wild coastal flowers,*

Cawsand (Walk 2) *(author)*
Sharp Tor (Walk 3) *(author)*

Rough Tor (Walk 5) *(author)*
The canal at Bude (Walk 7) *(W. Unsworth)*

especially in spring and summer.

Rame Head, once an Iron Age fortification, stands some 300ft above the sea and is a dramatic rounded headland with the little 14th century chapel of St Michael, said to be the patron saint of sailors, perched on its summit. There are legends told that a light was kept burning here to show sailors where the rocks were and also to guide them into Plymouth; an early lighthouse. It is certainly worth walking out to the headland because on clear days you can see back down the coast west to Dodman Point and nearby the wide sweep of Whitsand Bay. When Napoleon was captured he was on board HMS Belerophon when she anchored in the Bay. To the south you can just make out the Eddystone Light some 10 miles from the breakwater, now automated. I made a visit there filming for TV to talk to the last keepers of this famous light.

Walk back down from Rame Head and now there are decisions about the route to be made.

a. If you want to get back to Cawsand quickly, mainly on roads, then go up to the car park (one of the possible starts given) which is just to the left of the coastguard station. Follow the narrow lane to the church at Rame named after St. Germanus. *It has an unusual spire and a lot of slate is used on the building, parts of which date back to the 13th century. It is a delightful little church, well worth a visit, with a fine interior wagon roof and other wood carvings on the benches. There is no electricity there and services are held by candlelight.*

From the church the narrow Rame Lane will lead you through some pleasant countryside to Forder where you fork right and walk back down to Cawsand.

b. If you want to keep going a bit longer, after Rame Head keep left by the sign and walk along parallel with a stone wall across Queener Point outside the walls. After a while you will see Polhawn Fort below the path to the left, which is privately owned. *All around Britain there are similar defensive forts that were built in the 1860s when it looked as if the French would invade Britain. Plymouth has a ring of them. They cost a lot of money and of course they were never put to the test. Some have been converted into private houses and flats. There are fine views of the great curve of Whitsand Bay from here.*

By a tennis court go steeply down some stone steps to cross a track by the gate of the house. Go down more steps and through a gate to another track. Another decision now. You can turn right here and climb uphill to the road and walk to Trehill then over the fields to Forder on a public right of way and then finally back to Cawsand. However it is well worth keeping on along the Coastal Path north-north-west above Captain Blake's Point and Wiggle Cliff. The path climbs up to the car park (the other start) on the junction of the roads that go to Freathy and Wiggle where you will be going.

To the east of the hamlet of Wiggle you will see the Right of Way that leads across the fields to near Wringford Farm, then over the road at Forder Hill and on again over steep splendid countryside with superb views back to Cawsand.

3. MINIONS. HENWOOD. BEARAH TOR. KILMAR TOR. LANGSTONE DOWNS. THE CHEESEWRING. THE HURLERS.

Distance: Medium (just) 7 miles / 11$^{1}/_{4}$kms

Difficulty: Moderate

Maps: Pathfinder 1339; Landranger 201

Start: Minions, Map Ref. SX 261712. There is no car park here so please park carefully but there is plenty of room. This walk can also be started north of Henwood by the track leading onto the moor if you do not want or need to stop in the village of Minions, at Map Ref. SX 268741. Again careful parking needed.

There are shops, a post office, hotel and the highest pub in Cornwall. Like many villages in Cornwall this was once busy with miners and quarry workers who toiled nearby. Granite, rich tin, copper and lead ores were all transported by railway to Looe to be shipped all over the world.

From Minions set off up the left fork of the lane down to the small group of houses at Higher Stanbear. *Away to your right there are fine views over the wooded valley of the River Lynher which flows on down to the Tamar and the Hamoaze at Devonport and eventually Plymouth Sound. Kit Hill also stands out over 10kms away above Callington. To your left the mass of Stowe's Hill rears up above you.* Soon you will come to the pretty little village of Henwood. Keep walking on north and you will see, again to your left, the rocky peak of Sharp Tor. About $^{1}/_{2}$km after Henwood you will find the rocky lane that turns left (which

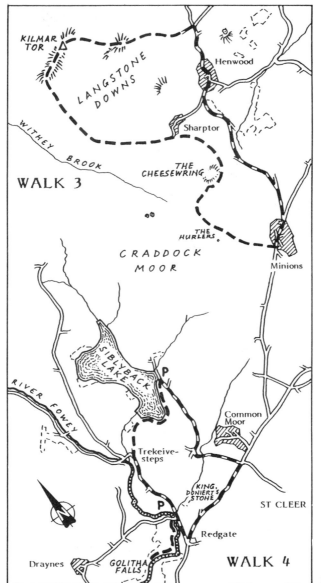

KILMAR TOR

Henwood

LANGSTONE DOWNS

Sharptor

WITHEY BROOK

THE CHEESEWRING

WALK 3

THE HURLERS

CRADDOCK MOOR

Minions

SIBLYBACK LAKE

P

Common Moor

RIVER FOWEY

Trekeive-steps

KING. DONIERT'S STONE

ST CLEER

P

Redgate

Draynes

GOLITHA FALLS

WALK 4

35

could be the start as I have suggested). Turn up this lane to start the gentle climb onto the moor. The track goes all the way to Bearah Tor climbing up through a mass of boulders with hawthorns and small oaks scattered across the bracken slopes. *There are also the remains of lichen-covered granite walls built by early farmers.*

The track leads right into the quarry on the side of the tor. You can scramble up to the right to the summit or walk off to the left to get round the jumble of rocks.

There is a wide sweep of flat moorland ahead of you now and on the other side there is the long rocky ridge of Kilmar Tor and a trig point at 390m, the third highest point of Cornwall. If you are something of a climber it makes quite an amusing scramble to go along the ridge of the Tor. *It is a fine viewpoint. Looking north you can see Trewortha Tor and Hawk's Tor as well as the lonely remote farm also called Trewortha near the section of the tor called King Arthur's Bed; it must have been uncomfortable! Towards the west you can make out the forests of Smallacoombe Downs where there are quite a number of prehistoric remains.*

Further back looking south-west you can make out Siblyback Lake, now used as a fine watersports venue. South you can see the coast near Looe.

The whole area around the Tor is known as Twelve Men's Moor. This name comes from the fact that the Prior of Launceston leased the land to 12 tin miners in 1284.

Swing south now and be prepared for wet feet the moor is fairly boggy here. If you want to it might be worth wandering off to your right to have a look at the settlements marked on the maps. Eventually you cross Langstone Downs and will find an indistinct path which leads to a gateway or you can look for the remains of the track of yet another extraordinary project. *It was proposed that a mineral railway should run across the moor towards Jamaica Inn and you can still make out the granite blocks that were to hold the rails; it was never completed.*

This will lead you down to North Wardbrook Farm. *Please keep any dogs with you on their leads - there are usually many sheep about - and shut the gates.* Walk on down the track from the farm until you get level with Stowe's Hill; don't wander off left to the hamlet of Sharptor. It is well worth climbing up to the summit of Stowe's Hill with its fantastic weathered granite slabs. *Again there are marvellous views from here, especially looking across the valley to the shapely rocky peak of Sharp Tor.*

You can't really miss the next point to aim for. It is the famous Cheesewring perched on the edge of a quarry. *This extraordinary tor was formed partly by weathering but also by the cooling, layer by layer, of the molten granite as it welled up from the depths, creating this strange effect of the granite slabs perched one on each other. The quarry and the Cheesewring is a well-known area for rock climbers.*

Mind how you go if you are not a climber but work your way to the southern edge of the quarry. Here you will see a small square open door leading into a pile of roughly assembled rocks. *This was the home of a notable eccentric called Daniel Gumb who lived here in this cave with his wife and nine children in the 1730s. Sadly the main cave was destroyed by the quarrying operations over 100 years ago but there is still a lot to see of interest. Daniel Gumb was called the 'mountain philosopher' and was a self-taught mathematician and astronomer. If you look carefully you can see where he carved geometrical shapes on the rocks nearby and here on the capstone, one which is the proof of Pythagoras's theorem. He also carved his initials D.G. and the date 1735. Deep in the rocks he divided his cave into rooms with granite furniture and it was said that the cave had a granite sliding door.*

Daniel Gumb was a fine craftsman and more of his carving can be seen in Linkinhome church where he carved his own epitaph with a great sense of humour:

> *Here I lie by the churchyard door;*
> *Here I lie because I'm poor.*
> *The further in, the more you pay.*
> *But here lie I as warm as they.*

He lived in the cave until his death.

Do not follow the track back directly to Minions but aim towards the west before turning south to walk down to the last point of interest, the Hurlers. *I am always intrigued by these mysterious Cornish stone circles and rows. They are of course a Bronze Age monument and are in the form of three stone circles. The legend says that they were men turned to stone for playing the Cornish game of hurling on the Sabbath. The same story turns up in West Penwith where you will find the Merry Maidens. This time it was the girls who got turned to stone for dancing on Sunday!* Follow the track back down to Minions and if you've timed it right the highest pub in Cornwall might be open.

The Hurlers with old engine house behind.

4. DRAYNES BRIDGE. GOLITHA FALLS. KING DONIERT'S STONE. SOUTH TREKEIVE. SIBLYBACK LAKE. TREKEIVE STEPS.

Distance: Medium (just) 8 miles / 12kms

Difficulty: Easy

Maps: (See p35) Pathfinder 1339; Landranger 201

Start: There is a car park near Drayness Bridge, Map Ref. SX 229690. You could if you wished start this walk at the car park on Siblyback Lake, SX 237707.

St. Cleer is the nearest village to the start of this walk with the usual amenities and it is well worth a visit. It is a typical moorland mining and quarrying village with the fine 15th century church of St. Cleer. Inside you will find a Victorian stained glass window showing 11 female saints. St. Cleer's well has an open-sided chapel built over it. North-east of the village is Trethevy Quoit, one of several in Cornwall which you will visit on other walks. It was a Neolithic chamber tomb with a huge capstone.

Draynes Bridge

Draynes Bridge is an ancient packhorse bridge built in the 15th century and was on one of the old trading routes into Cornwall, crossing the River Fowey that cascades down through the woods here. You will see the track that wanders down first south and then west beside the river. *The area here is a National Nature Reserve and you find quite a number of waymarked walks. There are not many large rivers inland in Cornwall but the Fowey is an exception and it is a delight to stroll down beside the rapids and cascades to Golitha Falls. They were much larger years ago but they used explosives to try to create a salmon ladder which was not a success. However in times of flood the raging water is very impressive. The woods are lovely at any time of year with the many beech trees. Bluebells and daffodils carpet the banks in spring while, in autumn, the beeches are a marvellous gold. As you approach the falls the sound of the water turns to a roar as the river tumbles down over the rocks and in and out of small gorges. The exposed roots of the trees and the ferns, mosses and lichens all create a green, almost tropical feel to this splendid valley.* Reluctantly now it is time for you to get back to the road to continue the walk, though this is a fine area to have a picnic if you wish and have the time.

Turn right at the road and walk down to the old cross at Redgate. (Those of you who have looked at the map might have seen a right of way running east below Bulland Downs to South Trekeive and if you wish to shorten the walk and avoid walking on the road you could take this, but you will miss seeing King Doniert's Stone. It starts just a little way north of the bridge opposite some houses. There is a sign by the gate.)

Going on, turn left at the crossroads at Redgate and walk along east for about ¹/₂ mile to the memorial. *These intricately carved stones were put up again, after they had fallen, by the Old Cornwall Society. They are a dedication to the 9th century Cornish king who was drowned nearby in AD 872. One of the stones has the Latin inscription "Doniert rogavit pro anima" (Doniert ordered this for his soul) carved on it while the other has an intriguing pattern cut into the granite.*

Walk on to the crossroads and again turn left. I'm afraid it's all road walking but it is a pleasant lane up to the little hamlet of South Trekeive. *Here you can't fail to notice the amazing collection of stone mushrooms in The Shippen. They were used in the old days to keep ricks up off the ground and even old barn buildings.*

Again those of you with maps will see another right of way that goes out across Bolland Down from here and will shorten the walk and lead you across to the dam, but you'll miss the lake itself. *This sunken track between low walls was one of the old 'green' lanes connecting remote farms and villages.*

If you go on, the road leads past an old cross and ahead lies Siblyback Lake.

Whatever one feels about reservoirs Siblyback does add extra dimension to this valley. A great number of birds live on or visit the lake and birdwatching is one of the activities that goes on here. You will also probably see people canoeing, windsurfing, sailing and angling and the lake has become an important recreational centre for Cornwall for both young and old. There is a sports centre and a small cafe where you can get a halfway refreshment.

Now follow the lakeside track past little sandy bays if the water is high, or mud if it is low, towards the dam. A steep flight of steps will take you down below the towering wall. *This dam holds back some 700 million gallons of water and the reservoir was opened in 1969.*

There is a signpost here that points you to Treivesteps. *You will* pass through an area where there were probably old fields and settlements that have long since sunk back into the landscape as you can still make out the remains of ancient walls.

The access track leads you back to the public road where you turn left again and walk on past Bulland Farm. You will soon be back at Drayness Bridge and your car.

5. ST. BREWARD. CAMPERDOWN FARM. LOUDON HILL. ROUGH TOR. BROWN WILLY. GARROW TOR. KING ARTHUR'S HALL.

Distance: Long 11 miles / 18kms
Difficulty: Moderate to Hard
Maps: Pathfinders SX 07/17 1338, SX 08/18 (1325); Landranger 200 & 201
Start: St. Breward, Map Ref. SX 099772. I have given the map reference of the pub, The Old Inn, which I thought might make a good start! As always please park carefully near here or anywhere in the village.

St. Breward is a sprawling village where you will find shops, a post office and so on. It was known locally as Simonward though I cannot find out why. By the whitewashed Old Inn there is an oddly carved stone and just north there is the lovely 15th century granite church dedicated to a 13th century bishop of Exeter.

Set off on the road that runs north-east to pass the farm called Palmers. Follow it round beside Treswallock Downs and then onto the unfenced moorland road to Camperdown Farm with its line of firs. On your right you will see the jagged rocks of Alex Tor and you will pass a sign that says 'No Through Road' and then another, 'Rough Tor. 43rd Wessex Division War Memorial'. You could of course drive to here but another sign makes it clear that you should go no further by car: 'Private Access. No Admittance. Fernacre Farm.'

This walk is rich in Bronze Age remains and also legends of King Arthur. There is an amazing Bronze Age stone circle made up of some 70 stones called Stannon Stone Circle and you might feel like diverting north

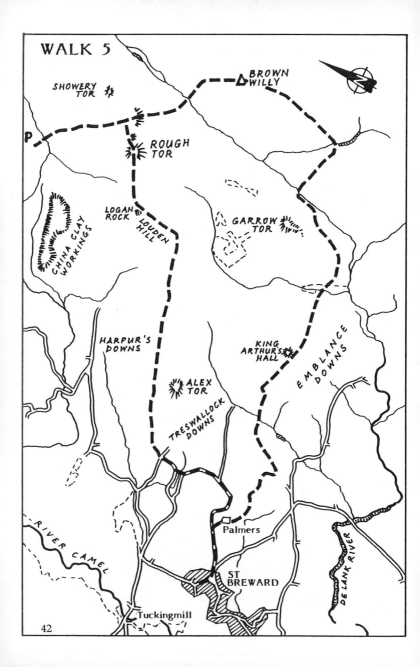

WALK 5

SHOWERY TOR

BROWN WILLY

P

ROUGH TOR

CHINA CLAY WORKINGS

LOGAN ROCK
LOUDEN HILL

GARROW TOR

HARPUR'S DOWNS

KING ARTHUR'S HALL

EMBLANCE DOWNS

ALEX TOR

TRESWALLOCK DOWNS

RIVER CAMEL

Palmers

DE LANK RIVER

ST BREWARD

Tuckingmill

to have a look at it; it's near the clay works you'll see to the north. You will also see Middlemoor Cross, one of nearly 400 granite crosses in Cornwall. They were usually set up on old routes for various reasons ranging from just a place to say a few prayers for the long and dangerous journey ahead or as a thanksgiving of some sort or even as a memorial to a saint or just a local dignitary; this one is probably medieval.

Still keeping north-east aim at Louden Tor and then, beyond, onto Rough Tor rearing up in the distance. *For me this is the sort of walking I really enjoy. The open moor lies ahead and on hot summer days the skylarks are minute specks in the blue sky, bubbling out their evocative song. Buzzards like huge moths wheel above you with their shrill kitten-like cries. Sheep and ponies live up here too and you may be lucky and see the rusty moorland fox trotting his arrogant way to raid some luckless farmer's hens or ducks.*

On Louden Tor there is a logan stone. There is another more famous logan stone near Porthcurno which you may visit on another walk but they are always fun to find and there are many in Cornwall. The one at Porthcurno does not rock but this one does; go carefully as you may end up as the unfortunate naval officer did at Porthcurno, having to put it back, at enormous expense, if you happen to dislodge it.

You probably won't want to walk all the way downhill to the north-west to look at a memorial stone but if you do feel strong then follow the path down for about 1km and a drop of 100m from Rough Tor when you get there. *Even if you don't walk down it gives me a chance to tell you another extraordinary Cornish story!*

On Sunday 14th April 1844 a young girl called Charlotte Dymonde set off to see some friends. She never turned up and nine days later she was found with a slit throat lying more or less where the memorial is today, at Map Ref. SX 139818. A wretched crippled boy called Matthew Weekes was questioned as he had told the police that he had seen Charlotte on the moor but he insisted that she was going to meet a certain Tom Prout. In great fear he ran away and tried to hide in Plymouth but eventually gave himself up. The murder caused an amazing furore and in the summer of the same year, 1844, 10,000 people gathered on the lower slopes of Rough Tor; an extraordinary day out for local people. The hat was passed round and enough money was collected to pay for the granite memorial you see today. Matthew Weekes was later found guilty of the murder and was hanged publicly outside Bodmin Gaol where 20,000 people had gathered. The mind boggles.

The Cornish poet Charles Causley tells the story also in his poem *The Ballad of Charlotte Dymond*:

> It was a Sunday evening
> And in the April rain,
> That Charlotte went from our house
> And never came home again.

The poem ends:

> And your steel heart search, Stranger,
> That you may pause and pray
> For lovers who come not to bed
> Upon their wedding day,
> But lie upon the moorland
> Where stands the sacred snow
> Above the breathing river,
> Where the salt sea-winds go.

Climb on now across the moor until you get to the clitters surrounding Rough Tor. To get to the top keep slightly left and you will probably see the bronze memorial to the 43rd Wessex Division.

Weird weathered granite on the summit of Rough Tor

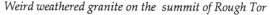

The land was given to the National Trust by Sir Richard Onslow as the memorial for the men of this regiment who died in the 1939-45 war. Apparently there used to be a small chapel here dedicated to St. Michael whose name turns up all over Cornwall, from the famous St. Michael's Mount to the little chapel which you might have seen on the walk round Rame Head. There he was said to be the patron saint of sailors, here he is supposed to be the patron saint of high places. I suppose he could manage both!

The summit of Rough Tor is spectacular with its huge flat granite rocks piled up to form the 'false bedding' that you might have seen at the Cheesewring. They form a mass of fantastic shapes and it doesn't need much imagination to turn them into giants' castles, dragons, hob-goblins and, of course, piskies, in your mind's eye.

All around are a large number of Bronze Age remains: cairns, walls of field systems, stone circles and settlements. If you have time you will probably want to divert and wander around looking at them. I always feel a strange prickling feeling on the back of my head when I am in these ancient places and I sense the presence of these early Cornish. What was life like for them? How did they manage to build the extraordinary stone rows and circles? Indeed why did they build them? Were they places of worship or commemorating one of their chieftains? Who knows? Cornwall is full of their mystery and several of the walks will take you to see their primeval labours. "Look on my works ye mighty and despair."

Across the moorland you will see Brown Willy (Bron Willi) and that is where you should aim now towards the south-east. You will come to a gate and a granite bridge that crosses the De Lank River, a delightful clear moorland stream at this stage of its life with elusive brown trout darting in and out of the stones. Roughtor Marsh is just north of here where the river rises. The source of the Fowey is only about a mile away to the west beyond Maiden Tor. It's interesting to see that the De Lank River flows down to join the Camel and then north into the Bristol Channel while the Fowey flows south to the English Channel, and yet they both rise within a mile of each other. Brown Willy, I suppose, forms the watershed.

A broad track leads you on to Brown Willy, the highest point in Cornwall at 1377ft/420m. Rough Tor (Row Tor) is only 60ft lower. There are more Bronze Age burial cairns here and an Ordnance Survey trig point. The views, as they were indeed from Rough Tor, are superb. To the *north you can just make out Lundy in the Bristol Channel while away to the south-east you can see Plymouth Sound. All around are brooding tors and the marvellous wild desolate moorland.*

Swing due south now from the summit over rough ground to Brown Willy Downs then aim just north of Butter's Tor. Watch out as it is pretty boggy in the bottom of the valley here where a small stream runs north-west back to the De Lank River. You might be able to pick up the traces of an indistinct path that reaches a ruin near the De Lank River. If the river is in spate you may have to retrace your steps back to the bridge you crossed earlier as you need to get across to the other side. *Above you here is the lovely Garrow Tor.*

Walk south past some more hut circles and ancient settlements through a small copse and then west towards King Arthur's Hall, a circular English Camp of the Iron Age. *The legend of Arthur yet again, and indeed we are not far from Dozmary Pool and Slaughter Bridge mentioned in the Introduction.*

Keep on west and then, by another ruin, the track turns south to the drive of the farm called Irish. The right of way goes through the farm to Palmers and hits the road you started out on, where you turn left back to the Old Inn and your car. *I think this is a really exciting and challenging walk taking you onto the high moors of Cornwall with tremendous views and all around the granite tors and mysterious Bronze Age remains.*

6. MORWENSTOW. VICARAGE CLIFF. HAWKER'S HUT. TIDNA SHUTE. HIGHER SHARPNOSE POINT. STANBURY MOUTH. STANBURY. TONACOMBE.

Distance: Long $3^1/_2$ miles / $5^1/_2$kms

Difficulty: Moderate

Maps: Pathfinder 1273; Landranger 190

Start: There is a car park near Morwenstow Church, Map Ref. SS 205153.

The church is well worth a visit. It has some magnificent part-Norman carvings on the porch of men and beasts. The interior is also very lovely. In the churchyard there is a wooden figurehead of the Caledonia *a Scottish*

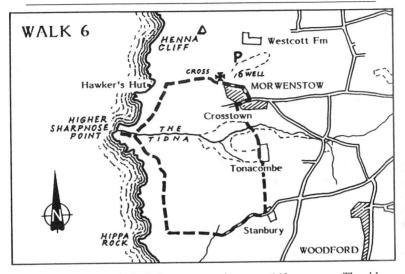

brig that was wrecked off the coast near here over 140 years ago. The old vicarage nearby has five extraordinary chimneys designed by Parson Hawker about whom I shall be writing in detail later on. They represent the towers of three Cornish churches where Hawker was the previous vicar, a college tower at Oxford and the tombstone of Hawker's mother. There are the two holy wells nearby of St. John near the village and St. Morwenna in the steep combe to the north. The village has the Bush Inn and places to have cream teas and you will also probably find a B&B in the area if you wish.

This walk follows the Coastal Path for some of its route but I have included it because of the bizarre story of the Rev. Robert Stephen Hawker but you must wait a minute to find out about him!

Set off on the path that leads to the cliff along the edge of Morwenstow Water, a steep combe to your right. When you reach the Coastal Path on Vicarage Cliff you must turn left to walk south. Great care is needed here and on other sections of this walk as the cliffs are very steep in places and if there are strong winds there could be real danger of falling or being blown off.

You will come to a sign that leads you the 30ft or so down to Hawker's Hut. *Hawker was an extraordinary and eccentric man born in 1803, the parish priest of Morwenstow from 1834 until a year before his*

47

Morwenstow Church

death in 1874. He searched for bodies after shipwrecks along the coast and then gave the unfortunate drowned sailors a Christian burial in his church. While they all had separate graves Hawker never put up headstones for them. He used to dress in sailors' jerseys and thigh boots and built this little hut of driftwood, where he used to sit smoking opium and meditating. He was also a fine writer and many poems and ballads were written here including The Song of the Western Men. *Tennyson and Kingsley both visited him in the 1840s; Kingsley of course had strong connections with the west country and Appledore and Westward Ho. The other interesting work for which Hawker is remembered is his incorporation of pagan festivals in a Christian form into his services. The best known is the celebration of the Harvest Festival. It is no wonder that in this small rural community, with gossip rife, that many weird and wonderful myths were told about him, many sensational and exaggerated but mostly untrue. I am sure that smoking opium didn't help! I wonder what the Bishop felt about this 'man of God'?*

The National Trust owns the hut and a lot of the land around here as you will see on the maps and by the notices. Climb back now from the hut and then follow the path until you have a steep descent to Tidna Shute. *There are many of these steep-sided combes on the Cornish coast where the little streams have cut sheer-sided valleys to reach the sea.* Cross the Tidna and get over two wooden stiles. Now it's a breath-gasping climb to get back up to the other side of the Tidna Shute or Water where you will find an old coastguard lookout, probably built in the war.

Off to your right you will see the exciting arête of Higher Sharpnose Point jutting out towards the west. It makes an airy and exciting detour to walk out to the end. But again do watch out if it is windy. *From the end you can look back along the edge of Vicarage Cliff and south to Lower Sharpnose Point and beyond. It is a marvellous vantage point. The rock here is known as the culm measures and is found all over northern Devon and Cornwall. It is a sedimentary shale and gives some excellent, if a little loose, rock climbing all along this coast.*

If you wish to cut the walk short here, you can drop back down to the bottom of Tidna Shute and follow the path on the north side of the stream back to Tidnacott.

If you are feeling strong keep on south across pretty rough country along the top of the cliffs beside quite a number of fields to your left. There are several stiles to cross but you will also see quite a few that have slipped down the cliff where wind and water have eroded the earth and rock away.

In the near distance you will have made out the sci-fi dishes and aerials of the Composite Signals Organisation Station that monitors satellites and much more, I suspect, and feeds the information to GCHQ. I suppose they are both sinister and beautiful and arouse both these emotions, rather like the wind farms further down in Cornwall.

Above Caunter Beach there is another chance to get back more quickly to the Bush Inn, if you wish, as a right of way will lead you over fields to Stanbury, where you can pick up the last part of this walk, but if your knees can take it then it's another steep descent. Drop down to Stanbury Mouth; quite a wild place. At the bottom leave the Coastal Path now and take the track that runs east back along inland leaving the stream on your right. After a while the track turns into a metalled road which you now follow.

At the historic old farm of Stanbury keep an eye out for the stile in the wall on your left opposite the buildings. This is a right of way that you can follow across two fields with a stile to climb between them. On the far side of the second field there is a gate that takes you to the lovely Tudor manor house of Tonacombe with its fascinating gateposts. *Built in the 15th century it has some magnificent features both inside and out such as courtyards and huge open fireplaces, wooden panels and a minstrels' gallery. It must have been one of the great thriving estates of this part of Cornwall.*

A track that can sometimes be muddy branches off to the left from the main farm drive behind the house. Go over the stile into a small field. There is a gate opposite which you go through and then keep on the right edge to get to Tidna stream, which of course you will have crossed at the far end, on the early part of the walk in Tidna Shute. *The culm measures are made up of very soft rocks and, as you have seen, these small streams have cut many deep valleys or combes and much of this walk and indeed a lot of the Coastal Path is a switchback up and down, in and out of them. But inland they form marvellous secret, wooded dells with a mass of wild flowers and this valley is certainly one.*

Go over the stream now and follow the path to the Bush Inn. If you have timed it right they might be open, so go down the left side of the pub and onto the road through a gate. Otherwise with great strength of will turn left for Morwenstow and your car.

7. BUDE. THE CANAL. RODD'S BRIDGE. HELEBRIDGE. SALTHOUSE. LOWER LONGBEAK. PHILLIP'S POINT. EFFORD BEACON. COMPASS POINT.

Distance: Medium 5¹/₂ miles/9kms
Difficulty: Easy
Maps: Pathfinder 1292; Landranger 190
Start: There is a large car park near the bridge on the outskirts of Bude, Map Ref. SS 209061.

Bude has been a popular summer holiday centre since Victorian times and the turn of the century, though I must admit I do not find it the most attractive of Cornish holiday resorts. It has a mild climate and splendid sandy beaches. Nowadays it is the surf that brings many tourists flocking here all the year round but especially in the summer when it can be very crowded. The Bude Surf Life Saving Club founded in 1953 was the first in

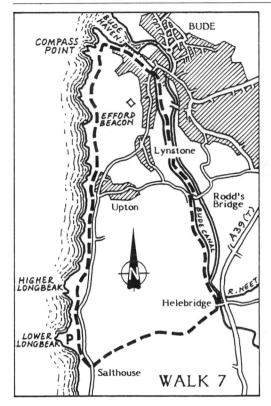

Britain. Obviously you will find here all the amenities of such a holiday town. With luck this walk will take you away from the masses.

Set off along the road towards a low squat but sturdy building with a little tower on it. *This small castle was built in the 1840s almost on the sandy beach and was the home of Sir Goldsworthy Gurney, a Cornish scientist who invented the steam blow-pipe and the Bude Light. One of the oldest houses in Bude, Ebbingford Manor, was owned and lived in by* another famous Cornish family, the Arundells.

Walk on now to the canal and the lock gates. *Bude was once a thriving port and vessels of 300 tons could be seen here in the 1900s in the canal with their masts adding to the picturesque setting. Lime, sand and seaweed were carried along the canal, opened in 1823, in barges to Launceston 30 miles away for fertilising the acid soils of the farms in this fine countryside. It was part of an ambitious scheme to link the Bristol Channel with the English Channel by cutting a canal down to link in with the River Tamar. In Walk 1 at Gunnislake there is an old long-abandoned canal there which was also part of this project. The coming of the railways,*

51

The main lock into Bude Canal

I suppose, killed the canals off. The long stone building here is an Historical and Folk Museum which is well worth a visit. It is open from Easter to October and you will find a huge amount of information about the area.

Walk over the lock gates to the eastern side of the canal and set off along the tow path. *There are quite a number of the old warehouses to be seen, reminding you of the days of the early industries here and the trade along the canal.* It is a peaceful walk along the tow path with the canal on one side and the river on the other. *Canals so often cut into countryside away from roads and villages and seem so quiet and tranquil. Wild flowers flourish along the banks and in the fields nearby while the only other people you will meet are other walkers, anglers and a few small pleasure boats on the canal. Towards the left is a nature reserve in the marshes where you might see there, and on the canal, herons, swans and many different waterfowl.*

At Rodd's bridge you must cross over to the west side of the canal and keep on down to Helebridge. *This was the limit of the larger barges in the early days and from here the cargoes were loaded into smaller tub boats which had to be hauled up inclines by winches run by steam or water power.*

At Helebridge the main stream of the River Neet flows in from the north-east. Upstream a mile or so is the small pleasant town of Stratton, famous as the birthplace of the 'Cornish Giant', Anthony Payne. He was born in the Tree Inn there and was over 7ft tall. He was a servant to Sir Bevill Grenville and fought with him at the Battle of Stamford Hill in 1643.

Cross the canal again before the bridge and go up onto the road which you follow for 100yds or so to the stile with a sign, on the left. Climb the stile and follow the path south-west across fields to Widemouth Bay with Black Rock standing gauntly out in the surf. It's not the most beautiful of Cornish seaside developments but you could always wander down for a cup of tea or an ice during the summer.

You are now back again on the Coastal Path which you follow north to Lower Longbeak. This is a fine viewpoint looking down on the sands of Widemouth Bay itself or north up towards the mysterious dish aerials that can be seen close by on Walk 6, near Mowenstow. There is an ancient tumulus here.

It's an exciting walk along the top of these culm cliffs and you will see many of the coastal flowers and plants mentioned in the Introduction.

It won't take you long to reach Phillip's Point, named after the farm just a little inland, and then on to Compass Point nearly at the end of the walk. By Efford Beacon, one of the early lights along this coast, you will see off to your right Ebbingford Manor, the old home of the Arundell family. There are fine views from here looking inland to Dartmoor with its thrusting tors and on clear days down to Trevose Head 30 miles away.

On Compass Point there is a strange octagonal building, a sort of lookout place on the cliffs from where there are again spectacular views both north and south along this jagged savage coast. It's no wonder that Parson Hawker had to recover so many drowned sailors from these shores. The entry into the Bude Canal must have been horrendous and there are no sheltering harbours within miles to run to if things were really bad.

Round the corner now, past the cliffs where there are some excellent rock climbs, and you'll soon be back at the entrance lock gates of the canal with the breakwater jutting out in an attempt to give some shelter. An early one was destroyed in a terrible storm in 1838. There are also the remains of the old lifeboat house. You can imagine the difficulties they must have had launching in storms from this rocky, treacherous coast.

Your car is just along by the river now. *I think that this is an extraordinary walk for contrasts. On the one hand you have the tranquillity and peace of the canal bank with all its wildlife, while on the other you have the ever restless sea and the sound of the surf and screaming gulls. I hope you enjoy it.*

8. CRACKINGTON HAVEN. CAMBEAK. THE STRANGLES. PENGOLD. EAST WOOD.

Distance:	Medium 4 miles/6¹/₂kms
Difficulty:	Moderate
Maps:	Pathfinder SX19; Landranger 190
Start:	The car park at Crackington Haven, Map Ref. SX 143968.

This is a walk of contrasts like the previous one. Once again I have gone onto the Coastal Path but with most of Cornwall being so close to the sea it's very difficult to plan walks that keep entirely inland. Crackington Haven is a remarkable little sheltered harbour lying deep in the mouth of the steep-sided valley of the small river that has cut down once again into the soft culm known here as the Crackington Measures. It was once a busy little port landing lime and coal to fuel the local limekilns so that lime could be spread on the acid soil of the local fields. The boats used to take away slate from the local quarries. You will find all you need in Crackington, especially in the summer when it can be very crowded as the sands are excellent here for holidays. Just up the road north of Crackington is the pleasant church at St. Genny named after St. Genesius who is said to have carried his head around after it had been cut off; another Cornish saint story!

Set off on the Coastal Path westwards from the harbour towards Cambeak. *This is a National Trust cliff as the sign tells you. I gather that a section of the cliff here was given as a gift in memory of pilots who were killed in the Battle of Britain.*

Below you to the right is Tremoutha Haven which, in 1836, was planned to be a harbour and a holiday resort called Port Victoria. They even passed an Act of Parliament to make it official and a railway was going to

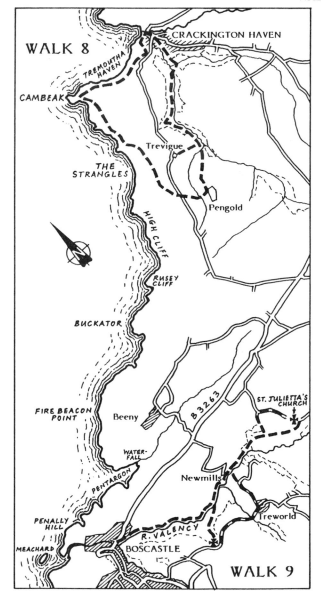

WALK 8

CRACKINGTON HAVEN

TREMOUTHA HAVEN

CAMBEAK

Trevigue

THE STRANGLES

Pengold

HIGH CLIFF

N

RUSEY CLIFF

BUCKATOR

ST. JULIETTA'S CHURCH

FIRE BEACON POINT

Beeny

B 3263

WATER-FALL

Newmills

PENTARGON

Treworld

PENALLY HILL

R. VALENCY

MEACHARD

BOSCASTLE

WALK 9

run here from Launceston. As you might expect, looking down on the hostile rocks, nothing came of it.

Once again you will see the erosion of the shale here by streams with small waterfalls cascading down to the sea through steep-sided valleys.

Cambeak is an impressive arête jutting out to sea but the rock is very loose and it could be extremely dangerous if you are not sure-footed or if a gale is blowing. The zigzag stratas of the synclines and anticlines are most impressive here and all along the cliffs in this section of the Crackington Measures.

Swing south now but if the winds are strong you can stay on a path in a little valley behind the point. After a while you will see yet another foiled attempt to make a harbour as there are the remains of an old quay.

Opposite the sinister jagged Samphire Rock take a look back and you will be able to see the rock arch of North Door. Samphire Rock is named after the small plants with fleshy leaves that grow on sea cliffs. They are good to eat and are used in pickles. The name comes from the French herbe de Saint Pierre.

The path follows south until you see some old quarries to your left when you are above the sandy beach of The Strangles. What a splendid name. They used donkeys to carry both sand from the beach and slate from the quarries. You can see the track they used to get down to the bay. It is said that Thomas Hardy used to come here with Emma, who was to become his wife, when he first met her at the vicarage at St. Juliot near Boscastle.

There are signs to show you the rights of way now across fields. Please follow them carefully and do not stray off the tracks. Go past the sign to an open field. Now aim diagonally to your right where you will see a stile in the corner. Beyond is the road where you turn left and then immediately right over another stile. Go right across the field and then aim for the stream at the bottom near Pengold Farm where you cross over and walk uphill to another sign. Here you are very close to the farm and another sign in the bank will point the way. Here you go left and ahead is a gate and another signpost. Go through the gate turning right, then left where you walk along the top of a steep field. Signposts will lead you down now to a delightful wooded valley.

From here you can divert to Trevigue Farm and a steep track

leads uphill left to this 16th century farmhouse. *It is owned by the National Trust and you can get cream teas here in the summer.*

To go on after your cream tea drop back down the track from the farm and now the path runs along the bottom of a charming steep-sided wooded valley and signs will lead you back all the way to Crackington Haven. *This valley is typical of the secret wooded valleys I wrote about in the Introduction with its woodland flowers and wildlife.* Towards the end you will have to cross the stream by a small bridge and after, turn left at a T-junction. You will then cross another stream and the path leads through a farmyard and down to the village.

As much as I hate signs, especially on open moorland, the whole of the last section of this walk is well signposted and uses ancient rights of way through farms and fields, which is to be applauded. I think one should respect this privilege.

9. BOSCASTLE. MINSTER WOOD AND RIVER VALENCY. NEWMILLS. ST. JULIETTA'S CHURCH. PENVENTON FARM.

Route A) Lesnewth. Treworld. Minster Church. Peter's Wood.

Route B) Newmills. Treworld. Minster Church. Peter's Wood.

Distance: Medium, almost Long. Route a) 7^{1}/$_{2}$ miles/12kms. Route b) 7 miles/11^{1}/$_{2}$kms

Difficulty: Easy

Maps: (See P55) Pathfinder 1310, 1325; Landranger 190

Start: Boscastle car park in the centre of the village near the Cobweb Inn SX 099914.

Boscastle is one of the few natural harbours in the 40 mile length of this savage north coast of Cornwall. It was once a thriving and important little port. The quay dates back to the 16th century and was built by Sir Richard Grenville in the time of Elizabeth I. The tortuous entrance to the harbour is so shut in by steep black slopes of wild land that it is hard to believe that the sea is just around the corner. Getting boats in under sail must have been a perilous and horrendous task and I understand that they used small rowing boats called Hobblers with eight oarsmen to tow the boats in, also

Old house on the quay at Boscastle

with the help of teams of men on the shore with ropes.

The name Boscastle comes from the Botterels or De Bottreaux family from Angers in France who built a castle here on a mound in the 1080s.

In spite of the ferocious entrance the port was busy, once again bringing in coal and limestone to make fertiliser, as well as other goods from Bristol to stock the little shops here and inland. They then exported slate from the famous Delabole Quarry inland. As it was with other ports, the railways killed off this harbour when they reached north Cornwall in 1893 with a station at Camelford.

In storms, if you walk out to the small quay, you may well be able to see the spray of a blow-hole in action at low water, towards the harbour mouth.

There seem to be links here with Napoleon. The jagged profile of a rock on the island off the entrance is said to be like Napoleon, while there is the Napoleon Inn here where they press-ganged young men into the army in the Nepoleonic Wars. Near the Old Mill is the Wellington Hotel. By the river where the walk will take you there is a house called Trafalgar. All very strange.

It is well worth wandering round the steep streets of the picturesque village with its old slate buildings and thatched cottages. There is an *information centre on the quay near a youth hostel. You will find all the amenities you might need but also a lot of people in the holiday season. Try to get here at another time.*

Just a little way up the Bude road is a small gate on your right that leads into the meadows and woods and after a while runs first beside the Old Mill Leat and then the River Valency. This is National Trust land. The path wanders along beside this delightful river that sparkles through the steep-sided valley with rocky outcrops jutting out here and there. There are gates to go through including a kissing gate so, depending whom you are with, use it as you will! There are more fields and meadows and then woodland.

After a while where the trees overhang the path you will see a footbridge on your right and this is the way you will return over it.

All this walk is full of memories and the romantic ghosts of Thomas Hardy and his wife Emma. In one of the tumbling waterfalls of the River Valency Hardy lost a cup while he was picnicking near here. He even wrote a poem about it after the death of Emma, called Under *the Waterfall.*

> *By night, by day, when it shines or lours,*
> *There lies intact that chalice of ours,*
> *And its presence adds to the rhyme of love,*
> *Persistently sung by the fall above.*
> *No lip has touched it since his and mine*
> *In turns therefrom sipped lovers' wine.*

Follow the river on now to Newmills and you will see a white-washed cottage. *Speculation has it that this was used by Hardy in his novel* A Pair of Blue Eyes *as the model for the home of Widow Jethway. Who knows? But without doubt Hardy loved this part of Cornwall and he describes the area in this novel.*

Ignore the lane off to the left and go through the gate with the sign that says 'Footpath to St. Juliot Church'. Fork left onto the narrow path that has another sign that tells you that this is the 'Public Footpath to St. Julietta's Church'.

Obviously you can take your choice with the name of the church. The local people call it St. Jilt, by the way, and the group of buildings near the church are called Hennett!

The path now is well waymarked but you must go through another kissing gate to follow the signs along a hedge to your left.

More gates and stiles until you bear left uphill to climb over the last stile into the churchyard.

Now we can unravel the question of names. The church of St. Julietta is in St. Juliot and it was founded by St. Julitta who was one of 24 daughters of King Brychan from South Wales. All his daughters were saints it is said; a likely story! But she came here in the 6th century and founded the church leaving her father ruling over the Brecons. Hardy wrote about the church as West Endelstow.

Hardy first came here in 1870 as an architect to plan restoration work on the church. He arrived on March 3 at Launceston and, in fact, only stayed four days. However he came back in August and the romance goes on from there, but you must wait until you walk up to Prevention Farm and the Old Rectory before you read more. It's interesting to see a sketch in the church that shows the 'six and thirty old seat ends' that were mentioned in the notes that Hardy made before he had them removed as part of his restoration work. I am sure there would be an outcry if such work was done today in an old church!

Leave the church and get onto the lane where you turn left. Walk on up to Penvention Farm and go left down a track. Shortly you will pass the Old Rectory on your right. *It was here that Hardy first met Emma Lavinia Gifford who was to become his wife. They both made notes about each other after their meetings.*

When Emma first met Hardy she noted that "he had a beard and a rather shabby greatcoat, and had quite a business appearance." There was a piece of blue paper sticking out of his pocket but this "proved to be the manuscript of a poem, and not a plan of the church" as, of course, she knew that Hardy was there to plan the restoration. His recollection of her was more romantic for she was the girl with "nut brown hair, grey eyes and a rose-flush coming and going."

Emma had come to live at the Old Rectory in 1868 where she was the house-keeper for her sister and the man she had married, who was the vicar of St. Julietta's.

After his visit in March 1870 and later in August Hardy returned often to the area to write his novel A Pair of Blue Eyes *which was published in May 1873. But obviously it was not only writing that Hardy did while he was in Cornwall for he proposed to Emma and they were married in London in September 1874! Emma died in 1912 and Hardy returned to the area several times from Wessex, the scene of so many of his other novels.*

Walk on now past the Old Rectory and then go left on the track to the corner of the field and follow down beside a hedge to your right. The gate ahead, which you go through, will then lead you down to the crosspaths you walked across on the way to the church.

Decision time now.

Route a) This is slightly longer and means quite a long walk in lanes rather than on paths or tracks. If you decide to take this route then cross over the crossroads and walk on down to the river where you will find a footbridge. The right of way then goes to the farm called Halamiling. From here a track will take you to the pretty hamlet of Lesnewth. *The church is tucked into a little valley and you can't really see it until you are right in the churchyard. Opposite the church there is a group of 17th century cottages which was probably a mill for grinding corn from the nearby farms.*

Set off now west along the switchback road towards Treworld. It's here you link up with Route b) so ignore the next section and pick up the information again when the alternative way arrives at Treworld.

Route b) When you arrive at the crosspaths, turn right and retrace your way back to Newmills. The path, as you will remember, runs along a steep bank and you will come to a little footbridge on your left with a ford nearby. Go over the bridge and through a gate that will lead you to a narrow track with hedges on either side and then on to the lane that leads to the house called Trafalgar that I mentioned in the information about Boscastle. Walk on now to Treworld, where both routes meet.

Here turn right and you can't avoid the road for a short while until you reach the little church of Minster. *It was built in a remarkable natural amphitheatre almost hidden and is both a delightful and dramatic setting. Built in the 15th century it stands where there was once a 12th century Benedictine monastery and that stood where a 5th century hermit had his cell. Nearly two thousand years of Christian buildings on this secret lovely site. It is well worth wandering round this church, especially in the spring when the churchyard is a mass of daffodils. You might just make out a carving of a pair of scissors on the west face of the tower. While inside there are several memorials and brasses worth seeing. One is for a child who died in the 16th century. Another remembers William Cotton whose wife died after 40 years of happy marriage in the 17th century. He was heartbroken and the epitaph says it all:*

> *She first departing, he a few weeks tried*
> *To live without her: could not and so died.*

You could, if you wished, walk back to Boscastle along the road back to the start through an area of the village called Paradise. But in spite of a chance to enter Paradise I prefer the route that goes back down into Peter's Wood and if it is SAINT Peter then Paradise might lie this way too!

Go through the gate into the wood; there are signposts. This is also National Trust land. At the fork go left into the woods. Another path will come in from the left as you wander back down to the footbridge that I mentioned in the early part of the walk on the way out. *Peter's Wood is a lovely wild wood with many oaks growing on the steep slopes. It was once coppiced: that age-old management of woodlands that was so common in Britain, sadly no longer so.*

At the bridge cross over and turn left to walk back to Boscastle. *It is no matter that you will have covered certain sections of this walk on the way out. I always feel that the views are so different facing the other way and even if they are not, the walk back again beside the River Valency is well worth it.*

10. CAMELFORD, FENTEROON FARM. TRETHIN. ADVENT CHURCH. PENCARROW. TRECLAGO. OUTGROUND MILL.

Distance:	3 miles / 5kms
Difficulty:	Easy
Maps:	Landranger 200; Pathfinder 1325
Start:	Camelford, Map Ref. SX 106837. There is a car park between the River Camel and the church.

A lot of people come to see the golden camel weathervane on the Town Hall but of course the name of the town comes from the Celtic Cornish cam pol *which means the winding river. It is a charming old town of slate-hung houses and slate roofs and a market dating from the 13th century that gained its importance from wool. The slate comes from the Delabole*

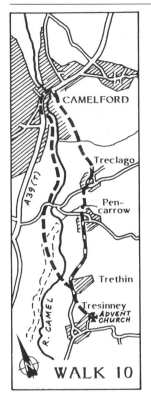

quarries nearby. *The town had two members of Parliament until disfranchised by the Reform Bill. There was a Lord Camelford, a notorious duellist who died in 1804 and it was the home of James Macpherson, the compiler of* Ossian. *About a mile north of the town is Slaughter Bridge that I mentioned in my introduction, which is the site of the legendary battle where King Arthur was fatally wounded. A hundred yards or so upstream from the bridge is a stone with a Latin inscription stating that this is King Arthur's tomb! Also in AD 823 there was another ferocious battle here between the Britons and the Saxons under King Egbert.*

Walk along Fore Street to the sign that points out the route to follow 'To River and Advent Church' which ducks down a passage. This will take you to a delightful path beside the River Camel. *There are water meadows and trees all around and as the whole walk is quite short it makes a lovely evening stroll on a hot summer's day.* You will have to climb a few stiles and go through a few kissing gates until you reach the old Fenteroon Bridge made of great slabs of granite that carries a small road. *This first section of the walk can be a little muddy.*

At the bridge turn right and walk a few yards up the hill on the road and then look out for the sign at the second gate which will lead you over two fields and a stile. The track then enters a charming wood that runs along parallel to the river and down to more water meadows that are a carpet of colour with flowers in the spring. *Ahead is a little footbridge in an idyllic spot tucked away in the depths of the secret Cornish countryside. You may be lucky and see herons and even that flash of blue lightning, the kingfisher.*

A steep climb will lead you up to the lane which you follow for a short while past Trethin Farm and then turn left to cross two fields up to Advent Church.

The Town Hall Camelford.

There are quite a few lonely remote churches such as this one in Cornwall built of local stone, standing rather forlornly in fields on their own. Advent Church is 15th century but with a Norman font. It has a fine roof with carved human faces in the middle section. The unusual name might come from St. Athwanne, one of those 24 daughters of the Welsh king Brychan who came from Wales; one wonders how many wives he had!

You could walk on south past the church to the lane where you turn right and then right again near the bungalow with the odd name of Viddy Vu to follow the lane to Trethin Farm.

Or turn and walk back down the hill to Trethin Farm and then keep going north on the narrow lane to the small group of pretty houses at Pencarrow. Bear slightly left and you will see the footpath just to the left of the farm that cuts across fields and down to a small plank bridge over a stream.

Much of this walk has been on private fields with public rights of way running across them so please respect this and keep to the paths and make sure your dogs, if you have them, are under control.

Climb up to the farm at Treclago and from here the route follows

Crackington Haven at sunset (Walk 8) *(W. Unsworth)*
Boscastle Harbour (Walk 9) *(author)*

Restormel Castle (Walk 12) *(author)*
The 15th-century bridge at Lerryn (Walk 13) *(author)*

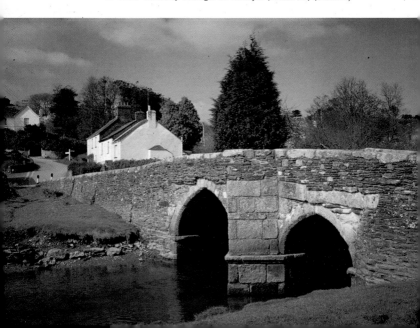

a track still north and then a path which crosses more fields before finally dropping down to a small footbridge at Outground Mill to cross a tributary of the River Camel. A narrow road takes you back past Highermead Park Hotel to Camelford. Turn left to your car.

This is a gentle beautiful walk into the exquisite Cornish countryside over many stiles and at least five little bridges. There are not many unusual, outstanding or historic things to see but the woods and water meadows are a delight to walk in, especially in the spring with the wild flowers and wildlife.

11. TINTAGEL. TINTAGEL CASTLE. BARRAS NOSE. SMITH'S CLIFF. WILLAPARK. BOSSINEY HAVEN. ROCKY VALLEY. ST. PIRAN'S WELL AND CHURCH. ST. NECTAN'S GLEN. HALGABRON. TINTAGEL. ST. MATERIANA'S CHURCH.

Distance:	Long (just) 7$^{1/2}$ miles / 12kms
Difficulty:	Moderate
Maps:	Landranger 200; Pathfinder 1325
Start:	Tintagel, Map Ref. SX 0588. Parking is always difficult in Tintagel as it is an extremely popular tourist village with all its connections, however dubious, with King Arthur. You'll have to find a car park wherever you can.

The shops are full of King Arthur souvenirs and nick-nacks and all the rest of holiday tourist trash; King Arthur's Cream Teas and Merlin's Icecreams! In fact the village is really named Trevena and it is the parish that is Tintagel. A lot of the village is full of modern horrors that have been built recently, but what you might call 'quaint' but also interesting is the National Trust property, the Old Post Office, a delightful Plantagenet manor-house dating back to the 14th century. It was the actual post office in the last century and has retained that character. Opposite is another interesting old dated building.

Alfred Lord Tennyson visited here in the 1840s and from that visit came, of course, Idylls of the King *and from then on the Arthurian legends have stuck. Earlier, Mallory had written* Morte d'Arthur. *Dickens, Swinburne and Thackeray also came here, another example of the love of the*

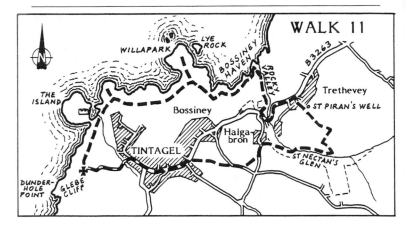

west country by the writers of the last century.

You can visit a Hall of Chivalry and King Arthur's Hall if you wish to indulge in the spirit of King Arthur! You will find 73 stained glass windows there depicting the coats of arms of the Knights of the Round Table and all their heraldry.

When you have had enough of the 'glitz' set off down the steep-sided valley signposted to the Castle and Castle Cove. You'll have to pay to visit the actual castle and, if you have time, it is probably worthwhile, for it is in a most spectacular site. In some ways it's almost better to view it from afar, as you will on this walk. You may have to fight your way up the steep steps with the hordes if you come in the holiday season.

As you might expect a lot of archaeological research has gone on here and it seems that there was a 3rd century monastery and a saint's 'cell' who was possibly St. Juliot; the monastery survived for several centuries.

When a fortified defensive castle was built is not clear but certainly the name could come from the Celtic, for the Cornish din-tagell *means fort of the neck. But records show that it was in the mid 12th century that a castle was built by Reginald de Cornwall, the illegitimate son of Henry I. The name then might have come from the Norman French* Tente d'Agel *which means Castle of the Devil. In 1337 Edward III invested his son Edward, who was to be known as the Black Prince, as Duke of Cornwall. The castle became his and he extended it and built a drawbridge between the mainland*

and the island where the castle stood. It is easy why it was said that three men could defend the castle against all attackers.

There is no proof that there ever was a King Arthur or indeed that he was ever here, except that study of the Anglo-Saxon Cronicles shows that he was a 6th century Celtic leader who fought against the Saxons. The sites of his battles and castles are claimed by Wales, Cornwall and even Wiltshire where an Iron Age fort is said to be Camelot. His death was at Camlann which could be on the Camel at Slaughter Bridge as I mentioned earlier.

I gather it was Geoffrey of Monmouth in the 12th century who started the story that Tintagel was Arthur's castle and from that germ of an idea, in the 15th century, Mallory wrote Morte d'Arthur and the legend was really under way. As mentioned before, Tennyson comes on the scene with Idylls of the King and that's it.

Though a little sceptical about it all I am always excited by the Arthurian legends; it's the exploitation of the tourists I dislike. The castle, Merlin's cave in the cove and the whole coast here has an air of magic and mystery and that thrills me.

Cross the footbridge to the right opposite the way into the castle and follow the steps of the Coastal Path up to the north and then along the cliffs to the zigzags that lead to Barras Nose. As I said earlier you get a most magnificent view of the castle from here. Once again follow the Coastal Path east, over Smith's Cliff.

It really is worthwhile turning left off the main path now to go out onto the headland of Willapark. Once again marvellous views from here along the coastline and, below, the savage rocks called The Sisters and Lye Rock. You'll find the grave of a victim of a shipwreck on Lye Rock at the end of this walk. Keep a watch out for seals bobbing their heads out of the water with limpid, inquisitive eyes to have a look round or lying basking on rocks; they breed near here. Seabirds wheel and cry around here and you will probably see fulmars, cormorants and auks. The end of the headland was an Iron Age fort with a ditch and a rampart to keep intruders out.

Back to the path and then steeply down to cross a small footbridge over the stream in Bossiney Haven. Down again until you reach Rocky Valley where you will find another footbridge. Don't go over it but turn right and walk up the true left bank of this stream. This is a lovely luxuriant wooded valley and I read somewhere that this was the last place where the rare red-billed Cornish chough nested until it became extinct in the county.

After a while you will see the ruins of an old mill and to reach it you cross a footbridge. If you go to the left of the building you will see, carved on the rock face behind, some strange mazes. *Nobody has really decided what age they are or what they mean. They could be Bronze Age, but the design is interesting in that it is the same as the Glastonbury Tor maze. As you might expect people who believe in 'Earth Magic' find them fascinating and full of meaning and power.*

From here walk on up the rocky valley and over another footbridge past Trevillet Mill and then a lane will lead you up to the road. Go left along the road and watch out for traffic on the hairpin bend.

Go past the Rocky Valley Hotel and turn right to St. Piran's Well and Church.

Yes, it's another Cornish Saint story coming up! St. Piran was a Celtic saint who came from Ireland to Cornwall. It's no wonder that he is the patron saint of Cornwall. He has a black and white flag which is also the flag of the men of Kernow who wish to have home rule for Cornwall. The story goes that he was chained to a millstone and thrown into the sea off a cliff by the Irish. As he hit the water, the storm and the huge seas that had been raging died down, the sun came out and the water was like a millpond. The millstone floated and St. Piran calmly set off for Cornwall! His well that you will see is shaped like a beehive with a cross on top.

The church may date from the 15th century but part of the building was a farm until 1942. There is some stained glass which shows St. Nectan in his glen, where you will be walking in a while, and there is a charming small chapel in the garden.

Walk on now on the path past the church. If you want to cut off a corner you can take the path south-west that is signposted 'St. Nectan's Glen'. The more interesting route however is to take the lane that runs south-east. It goes round two sharp right-angled bends and eventually, at its end, leads you to the Hermitage and St. Nectan's Kieve or waterfall. *I am afraid that like Tintagel Castle you will have to pay to visit the Kieve.*

And here is yet another Cornish saint story. St. Nectan is said to have lived here with his two sisters. Nearby was a small chapel that had a silver bell. The local belief was that when the local fishermen, out at sea, heard the bell ringing they knew that the saint was praying for them and looking after them. The legend continues that, when he died, his sisters put his body in

an oaken coffin and after diverting the waterfall they buried it under a great
slab of rock in the pool where the waterfall ends after its 50 foot plunge. In
the coffin were all the saint's treasures including the silver bell. Nowadays,
if bad weather is coming, it is said that the good people of Tintagel can hear
the bell tolling below the waterfall!

The story goes on that in the 18th century some local miners set about
trying to find the bell and the other treasures by once again diverting the
waterfall. As they searched around in the pool they heard ghostly voices
telling them that they would never succeed. As you might expect they
threw down their picks and shovels and fled in horror!

St. Nectan's sisters went on living in the glen after his death and rather
like the old ladies of Snailies House at Bellever on Dartmoor, they lived on
snails, fish and berries, growing more and more eccentric and quite clearly
in league with the Devil!

Not surprisingly, of course, the glen is haunted, not only by the sisters
but sinister monks are said to glide about in the gloom! There is a link here
back to the Rev. Hawker of Morwenstow whom you may remember from
Walk 6. He wrote a series of poems called The Echoes of Old Cornwall
in which he recounts the story of the weird sisters of St. Nectan.

Back to the walk. Go on now down the glen to the right which
is like a miniature rain forest. *The sun has a job penetrating to the bottom
of the deep and narrow gorge and you will find ferns, mosses and lichens
growing here.*

After about 440yds you will cross a footbridge and soon after,
another two. A kissing gate will lead you to a field which you walk
over to the road. Follow the road by turning left for some 220yds
until you come to a stile on your right. Climb over into the field and
then aim at the houses on the far side of the field. Another stile and
after going between two houses you will get onto another road
where you turn right. After another 220yds go down a small lane
and once again over a stile that will take you into a field. A few more
stiles and fields will get you back to Tintagel. *You may notice a mound
on your right as you cross the last field. This is marked on the maps as
Bossiney Castle and is the site of a Norman bailey castle. By the way, all the
rights of way on this section of the route are also clearly marked on the
1:25,000 map of the area.*

If you've parked at the east end of the village you may be
tempted to call it a day but I would urge you to add just a short

distance to the walk (or you could even cheat and drive there!) by taking the fourth turning left up a lane to have a look at St. Materiana's Church. On the way you will see a fine dovecote.

It is perhaps one of the most interesting and outstanding little churches in Cornwall. It is early Norman, built during the end of the 11th century, even with some Saxon influence from earlier. Indeed the Celts also probably had a church here before that. St. Materiana was yet another Cornish saint, a princess who came from Wales probably in about AD 500.

Inside, those of you who are interested in old churches will find a large number of remarkable and fascinating things to see: two Norman fonts, a bowl that is said to have been taken from St. Joliot's Chapel in Tintagel Castle, a 15th century rood screen, a triple lancet window, some really beautiful original stained glass, a Roman stone used once to sharpen farm implements, brasses from 1430 - the list goes on and on. It's well worth a visit. And one final sad reminder of the savage wild coast of this part of Cornwall: in the churchyard is the grave of a very young ship's boy, Domenico Catanese, who died when his ship the Iota *was wrecked on Lye Rock in 1893.*

If you would like to have another fine view of Tintagel Castle then walk north along the cliff path to the few ruins on this side of the chasm to look back at the castle on the island. Finally follow the path back down to the bottom of the steep valley that you came down at the start of the walk. You can then return back up the track to the village.

Otherwise you can walk back down the lane that you came along to reach the church to get back to your car and the village.

I find this one of the most exciting, fascinating and interesting walks in Cornwall, full of Cornish legends, contrasts and delights. I hope you will too.

12. BODMIN PARKWAY STATION. RESPRYN BRIDGE. LANHYDROCK HOUSE. KATHLEEN BRIDGE. RESTORMEL CASTLE. LOSTWITHIEL.

Distance: Medium 4$^{1}/_{2}$ miles/7$^{1}/_{2}$kms

Difficulty: Easy

Maps: Landranger 200; Pathfinder SX 06/16 and just onto SX 05/15

Start: Bodmin Parkway station, Map Ref. SX 110640. I have not been able to find many walks that follow some of the delightful Cornish rivers and as they are obviously linear here is a walk that does not return to the start but works its way down the River Fowey. But if you cannot get someone to pick you up at the end it is possible to use the railway to get back to where you parked your car at Bodmin Parkway station. By the same token it is possible to start in Lostwithiel and return there by train at the end. It needs careful checking with the train times as they are fairly few and far between that stop at both Bodmin Parkway and Lostwithiel.

If you arrive by train set off from the 'down' side platform and as you leave the station turn to your right and you see two tracks: one leads to the car park to the right and another goes off left. If you come direct from the car park walk down to this junction. Between the two tracks you will see a small gate which you go through onto a path that leads you under the railway and by many laurels down to the River Fowey.

Go over the river by a small bridge and walk left downstream through water meadows and woodlands. *This is a lovely stretch of river and is well known by fishermen. It is owned by the National Trust who have produced a fascinating map of this section of river, aimed mainly at fishermen, with the names of all the woods and pools.* You will pass Corner Pond and Claypipe Pool before you come to Respryn Bridge, one of Cornwall's finest oldest bridges.

From here I suggest that you walk up the avenue of beech trees to Lanhydrock House as this is a short walk and you should have plenty of time. *It is open from March to October but if you can get there in late spring, April or May you should find the masses of beautiful*

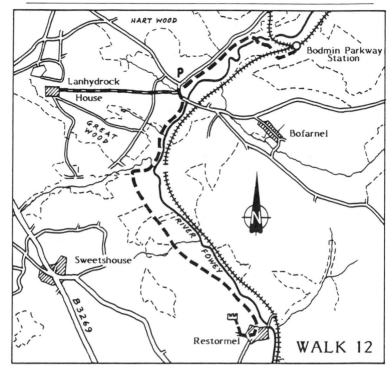

rhododendrons, camellias and azaleas in full bloom; they are quite a sight.

Lanhydrock belonged to the Augustinian Priory of St. Petroc which was near Bodmin before it was taken by Henry VIII in 1539. In 1620 it was bought by the Robartes family where they remained until they gave it to the National Trust in 1953 together with the surrounding 400 acres of woods and parkland. The early branch of the family in the early 17th century made their fortune by trading and became one of Cornwall's influential landowners. Lord Robartes was one of the leading Parliamentarians of the mid 17th century. It is interesting to note however that it was, in fact, held by the Royalists in the Civil War and, just down the road where you will be walking, Lostwithiel was held by the Cromwellians.

As you approach the house it looks Tudor but sadly most of the 17th century house was destroyed in a disastrous fire in 1881; only the north

Respryn Bridge one of Cornwall's oldest and finest.

wing and gatehouse were left of the 1651 house. What you see is a Victorian copy in the Tudor style. If you go in you will gain a fascinating idea of what life was like in Victorian times with the 'upstairs and belowstairs' clearly illustrated. You can get snacks and meals here too served in the old servants' quarters; to keep you in your place of course! Her Ladyship's room and the Long Gallery as well as many other rooms are all worth a visit. Up on the hill you will find the 15th century church of St. Hydrock.

Back now to Respryn Bridge where you cross the river and climb over a wooden stile to walk down the east or true left bank of the River Fowey. *This is really a most beautiful and tranquil stretch of river with trees all around. Keep your eyes open for herons, dippers and kingfishers; you might be lucky.*

Kathleen Bridge was built by the National Trust and you cross over when you get to it to reach the west or true right bank of the river. On the other side turn left downstream. After a while the path climbs up from the river to a small country lane which you follow left parallel to and above the river.

As you walk on, the valley begins to widen and as well as oak woods there are now fields. Soon you can make out Restormel

Castle on top of a hill covered with fir trees. It is worth wandering up the steep road to have a look round this splendid Norman keep.

Restormel Castle was one of the three main castles guarding the most important routes into Cornwall in Norman times. The others are at Trematon, just over the Tamar, and Launceston. When you consider that all that remains here, well preserved and restored, is the keep, it makes you realize just how huge the castle must have been, for the keep is over 100yds round. It is in a fine defensive position atop the hill.

All that is left now is to walk on down the road past the fir plantations that belong to the Duchy of Cornwall towards Lostwithiel that you can see ahead with the spire of St. Batholomew's Church standing out above the town.

You will pass by, between the castle and the town, what was the biggest iron mine in Cornwall. *The ores were taken by a tramway down to the river where they were loaded onto barges which were then sailed down to Fowey where the ore was shipped to the smelting towns in the industrial north and abroad.*

If you would like to find out more about Lostwithiel, which indeed is worth visiting, have a look at the introduction to walk 13. I hope you catch the train back to your car without too much delay or that you have managed to get someone to meet you here, but I am sure you will agree it is an unusual and marvellous walk down the River Fowey.

13. ST. WINNOW. GREAT WOOD. MIDDLE WOOD. LERRYN. ETHY.

Distance: Long (just) 7$^{1}/_{2}$ miles / 12kms

Difficulty: Easy

Maps: Landranger 200; Pathfinder SX 05/15

Start: St. Winnow, Map Ref. SX 116570. This little church is on the River Fowey south of Lostwithiel which is an attractive little market town.

Lostwithiel was the capital of Cornwall for a short while during the 13th century until Launceston took over. It was on an important road into Cornwall as the lowest bridge over the River Fowey is here. Tin and wool made it rich and it had the Stannary Court here and the seat of the Duchy

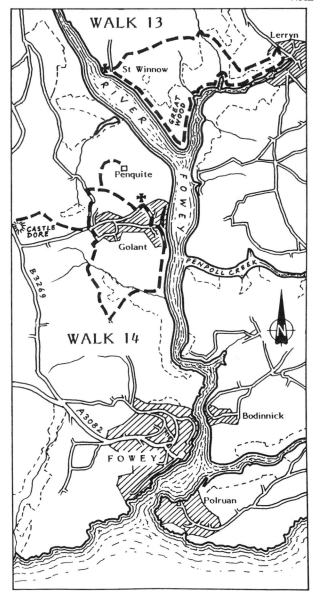

Parliament. There are quite a few fine Georgian houses and narrow passages, one of which leads through an arch in the walls of the 13th century Old Duchy Palace. St. Bartholomew's Church, also 13th century, has an unusual octagonal spire similar to those seen in Brittany. There is an interesting local history museum in the Guildhall which was built in 1740.

This is a walk that, while it does not pass or go to any places of great historical interest or is connected with any saints or castles, I find very worthwhile. It is a gentle walk through glorious woods by creeks and the estuary of the River Fowey to a delightful little hidden village with a good pub; an important point!

There is a saint however at the start of the walk: St. Winnow, or St. Winnoc as he was known in AD 670 when he came here to build a thatched oratory. He was a great traveller because he also went across to Brittany and founded another oratory at Plouhinec and then on to Berrges St. Vinoc near Dunkirk where he did the same. A handmill seems to have been his symbol because one of the stained glass windows in the church shows his carrying one. The walls of the church here were built in Norman times but the tower and other parts were built at the end of the 15th century. There is also some fine 16th century glass which shows how people dressed at that time. There is a lot of outstanding carved wood in the church including a rood screen and pulpit, not to mention the ends of the pews which will keep you wandering and looking for quite a while. If you go into the Lady Chapel you will find a splendid epitaph for a William Sawle who died in 1651:

> When I was sick, most men did deem me ill.
> If I had lived, I should have been so still.
> Praise be the Lord, that in Heaven doth dwell,
> Who has received my soul - now I am well.

In the graveyard there is the tomb of someone who lived at the Earl Chatham, Bridgend, Lostwithiel, who died in 1902. There is a pub with this name near the 15th century bridge in Lostwithiel. Apparently the first William Pitt was the owner of the great parkland estate and house of Boconnoc just north-east from here and he later took the title of Lord Chatham. Obviously the pub was named after him as one of the local landed gentry.

The little church of St. Winnow was used by the BBC in their Cornish series Poldark for the setting of a wedding of that period.

Set off now through the little gate in the far corner of the churchyard. For a short while you must walk along the foreshore past a boathouse. By the stream, after a hundred yards or so, look for a stile that will lead you into a field. On the far side there is another stile by a hedge and this will take you into the woods; look for the sign.

This is Great Wood and what a majestic place it is with tall ancient beeches, oaks, chestnuts and ash. Quite a number of these west country estuaries have dense woods running to the water's edge almost like a jungle.

The path will lead you round to the north as you leave the River Fowey and follow the creeks and inlets of the River Lerryn.

After the second creek you must follow the lower path to the right before a larger track which goes up the creek to St. Winnow Mill. A small wooden footbridge takes you over the stream at the head of Tregays Creek and you will drop back down to the river at Ethy Rocks, a tranquil and lovely spot.

Soon the village of Lerryn will appear round the corner after you have seen some old buildings on the far side of the river. Walk on past some delightful cottages to turn left past more cottages which

The stepping stones at Lerryn at low tide.

have been whitewashed. A turn right will take you past a green house and on to the charming 15th century bridge. The creek is tidal here and at low tide you will see some stepping stones across the River Lerryn as well as the bridge. Soon you will come to the main part of this idyllic village with its limekiln and stores and also where you will find the Ship Inn which makes a welcome halfway stop, if you have timed it right!

I read somewhere that there is a strange prehistoric earthwork that runs from Lerryn to Looe, rather like the reaves you find on Dartmoor. Nobody is quite sure who built them or why. They could have been boundaries or of some religious significance but whatever they are the toil, organisation and back-breaking work that must have been needed to build them is beyond imagination; there were no JCBs or bulldozers in those prehistoric days! There is a marvellous local saying that goes "One day the devil, having nothing to do, built a great hedge from Lerryn to Looe."

If you can drag yourself away from the Ship Inn it is time to set off back to St. Winnow. Go back to the green house and the whitewashed cottages where you turn right up a steep lane. You will see a road called Lerryn View on your left and if you walk to the far end of the estate you will find a stile to your right by the last building. Climb over the stile and walk back across the fields below Ethy. The rights of way are all well marked on both Pathfinder and Landranger maps.

After a wooded section the path turns westward and drops back down to the River Fowey. You will see the little tower of St. Winnow church squatting below you as you finish this glorious circuit.

14. ST. SAMPSON'S CHURCH. GOLANT. BODMIN PILL. PENVENTINUE. LANHERIOT FARM. TORFREY. (CASTLE DORE). THE SAINT'S WAY.

Distance: Medium $3^1/_2$ (4) miles/$5^1/_2$ ($6^1/_2$)kms
Difficulty: Easy
Maps: (See Map P75) Landranger 200; Pathfinder SX 05/15
Start: Near St. Sampson's Church, Golant, Map Ref. SX 121553. There is room to park on the right just before the bend in the road where you will see the church to your left.

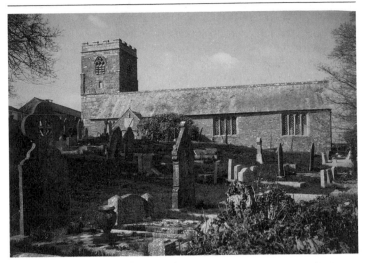

St Sampson's Church

St. Sampson's Church is well worth looking round and you can do that either at the start of the walk or at the end. Sampson was another saint from Wales who came across to Cornwall to convert the pagan tribes, led by Gwedian, to Christianity. He was said to be King Arthur's nephew as his mother was Anna of Gwent who was Arthur's sister; you can't get away from King Arthur! Gwedian and his tribe were ready converts when Sampson brought back to life a boy who had been killed falling off his horse and later when he killed a monstrous snake that lived in a black hole down by the River Fowey. Gwedian was so impressed that, on Sampson's command, he built a monastery where the church is today, before Sampson, like so many other Cornish saints, went on his way to Brittany. The church here now was probably built around 1509. There is a pulpit made of old carved bench-ends. There is also a holy well which you will find to the left of the porch.

Set off down the hill to Golant. At the crossroads it is worth turning left to walk down beside the harbour and the old trading quay before turning right again by the Fisherman's Arms. (You can have that pint later!) *The old name of picturesque Golant had a lovely sound. It was known as Golenanta in Elizabethan times and before. You will see the railway line on the far side of the harbour that sadly no longer carries passengers down to Fowey, but what a beautiful journey it must have been until Beeching got his hands on the line.*

At the T-junction turn left. After a while the road ends and you now must go straight on along the path. Off to your left is both the railway line and, of course, the River Fowey.

Keep an eye out left for a view up Penpoll Creek on the opposite side of the river. If you look at the maps you will see the name St. Cadix (how many more of these curious Cornish saints are there?!) at the head of a St. Cyric's Creek. This is the site of a priory founded by St. Cadoc from Wales.

Keep on south now until you reach Bodmin Pill with Colvithic Wood on the far side. *The strange word Pill is Celtic and means a tidal creek. Apparently in medieval times this little inlet was used by quite large trading vessels owned by rich merchants from Lostwithiel and Bodmin who came in here to avoid paying their harbour dues at Fowey. Nothing has changed!*

The rights of way are clearly marked on the maps from here and the path is fairly easy to follow. Cross the stream on stepping stones at the head of the Pill and then turn right to climb up through the wood. Follow the path with a hedge on your right until you go through two gates that will lead onto the road. Here turn right and go through the gate leading to Lanheriot Farm.

You will appreciate and respect the fact, I am sure, that this is a public footpath that leads through a working farm. The sign will tell you where to go along a track.

A small footbridge will take you over the stream that runs on down to Bodmin Pill. Soon the track becomes a surfaced road where you turn left and walk on to the crossroads.

You will have noticed that, in the distance given at the start of the walk there are two in brackets, one of which is slightly longer. I felt that some of you might like to turn left at these crossroads to look for the right of way on your right that will lead you over the fields to Lawhibbet Farm and then on to have a look at Castle Dore, a fine example of a typical mound of an Iron Age earthworks with its ditches and walls.

The whole area is full of further legends and myths. St. Mark of Cornwall is said to have lived at Castle Dore and Mark was the uncle of Tristan who, of course, was the tragic lover of Iseult. To get back to St.

Sampson's Church you must retrace your steps back to the crossroads.

You will notice a driveway on your right that leads to Penquite Youth Hostel. This must be one of the most splendid youth hostels in the country as it is situated in a beautiful Italianate stucco mansion built by a Colonel Peard in the 1840s. It is said that Garibaldi stayed here.

If you didn't walk out to Castle Dore you will notice it away to your left on this section of the walk. Soon, after about 500m, you will see a stile on your right with a yellow waymark sign telling you that this is the Saint's Way. I shall be giving the whole route for this later on in this book but for now you must follow it for a short distance back to St. Sampson's Church. It is quite a complicated section of path with four stiles to climb over but easy to follow. You will also cross the driveway to Penquite mansion and you might care to wander up to have a look at the lovely building before returning to the Saint's Way and finally going through a gate to reach the church and your car.

And what about the Tristan and Iseult legend? Well there used to be the Tristan Stone in St. Sampson's Church that was taken away and now stands by a crossroads about a mile north-west of Fowey. It is 6th century (Mark was indeed king of Cornwall in the 6th century) and on it is the Latin inscription "Drustanus hic iacit Cumomori filius" - Here lies Drustan (Tristan) son of Cunumorus. It must at one time therefore have marked the grave of Tristan who, as you will remember, had the tragic love affair with Mark's wife, Queen Iseult. One of the stories goes that Tristan lost both his parents when he was a child and was brought up by his uncle Mark. While Tristan was away fighting in Ireland he was wounded and was nursed and cherished by the beautiful Iseult, the daughter of the Queen of Ireland. When he returned to Cornwall he told his uncle Mark of the beautiful princess there who had looked after him. Mark set out to woo Iseult and indeed married her but she was in love with Tristan as he was with her. Full of remorse and unhappiness Tristan was banished to Brittany. The story goes on and I am sure you will want to find out more. He was of course one of the knights of the Round Table. King Arthur again! History, legend or fact? Who knows? Wagner please note!

15. LUXULYAN. LUXULYAN VALLEY. CARMEARS WOOD. PONTS MILL. TREFFRY VIADUCT.

Distance: Medium 4 miles / 6½ kms
Difficulty: Easy
Maps: Landranger 200; Pathfinder SX 05/15
Start: Luxulyan Church, Map Ref. SX 052581. Careful parking is needed here but there is room opposite the church.

Luxulyan is another of these small Cornish villages tucked away in the

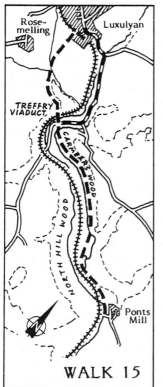

depths of the secret countryside off the main roads though it is on a railway line so you could come here by train. There is a pleasant pub and some interesting cottages. The church of Saints Cyriacus and Julitta is 15th century and like the cottages is built of locally mined granite. Indeed the village was well known for its granite quarries in past times. At the lower end of the village there is a Holy Well dedicated to St. Cyor which has a stone canopy over it and now, I'm afraid, no water.

Set off down the road leaving the church on your left. A small bridge will take you over a stream and soon after you take the right turn down the lane signed 'Luxulyan Valley'. Where another steep lane is seen to your left go in through some granite posts before climbing through the trees up to a leat. You now follow the leat south-east down the valley.

This valley is a favourite walking spot for local people, especially in the spring. It is richly wooded with its slopes covered with trees, mossy boulders, bracken and a great many different species of fern. There are a vast number of blocks and boulders, some of enormous size. There is one known as the Giant Block, said to be the largest in Britain. Scattered among the boulders of ordinary granite there are some fine specimens of a pink porphyritic rock known as Luxulianite. Out of one of the huge blocks of this rock weighing 70 tons was hewn the sarcophagus of the Duke of Wellington, now in St. Paul's Cathedral.

After about a mile along the leat you will see the remains of an ancient waterwheel and then an old incline crosses the leat. *You can still make out the granite sleepers on this, the Carmears Incline here, on which trucks carrying minerals that had been crushed at Ponts Mill used to run. It was built and was used in the 1840s and a wire rope hauled the trucks up the steep 1 in 10 slope.*

It's worth walking on down to the right to have a look at Ponts Mill, passing under a small bridge as you go.

You must return now the way you came but this time walk on up the old incline and after a while it goes left where you will see another leat that runs above and parallel to the one that you followed on your outward journey. You walk back along this higher leat.

After about a mile the leat goes underground and you will find the mighty viaduct ahead. *It is known as the Treffry Viaduct, as it was built in 1839 by local mine and quarry owner Joseph Treffry, and it carried a mineral line and aqueduct across the valley and on down to the port of Par.*

You now cross the viaduct, pausing to look over the edge if you have a good head for heights and at the marvellous views up and down the wooded valley below. The leat is now on your right. After just over 100yds the path crosses another leat (what surveying and engineering skills must have been used for all these leats) and you will see some steep stone steps which you go down to your left. When you see a tunnel on your right you must follow the path away from it to cross two small bridges.

Once again the rights of way are clearly marked on the maps and they will show that you turn right onto a wider path and cross another bridge over a leat. A stone stile will take you on to a track until you see a granite post to your left. There are more stone steps that take you over a wall on your left. There are a couple of fields to cross, a gate to go through and a track to cross before you see the

The Treffrey Viaduct

path that leads you back to the church to end this unusual walk. *Those of you who know Brittany might have visited Huelgoat. I find the woods and the great granite boulders in the Luxulyan Valley very similar to the extraordinary features near this delightful little Breton village.*

16. MOUNTJOY. LADY NANCE WELL. COLAN. PORTH RESERVOIR. TREGOOSE. BOSOUGHAN.

Distance: Medium 4 miles/6¹/₂kms

Difficulty: Easy

Maps: Landranger 200; Pathfinder SW 86/96

Start: Mountjoy, Map Ref. SW 872604. Once again please park carefully in Mountjoy, or you could get here by bus from Newquay, St. Austell or Truro as the A392 passes just south of the village which is a bus route.

Set off along the road to Colan but on the outskirts of the village go off down a track to your left past a cottage. When the track ends

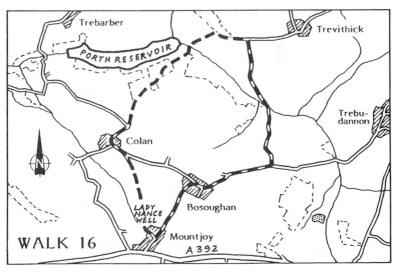

climb over a stile to your left and drop down to a small gate in the far left-hand corner of the field. Go through the gate and cross a stream. You will then see a path made of concrete blocks. Turn right along a lane to have a look at Lady Nance Well.

The water of Lady Nance Well, like so many other wells, holy or not, has special properties and it was said that it would cure eye diseases. Nance is probably a Celtic word meaning a stream like the Welsh word nant. *Local legend has it that the nearby villagers would come here on Palm Sunday with their palm crosses and throw them into the well. The idea was that if the cross floated all would be well and they would have a prosperous year with no illness but if it sank they could have a bad year and might even die!*

Go back along the concrete blocks to the field where you turn left through a gate. The path is obvious now and marked on your maps. Go through another gate and along by a hedge until you reach a gate in the corner of the field which leads to a track. This in turn takes you to the road where you turn left to walk along to the church.

St. Colan's Church is another of these squat little granite Cornish churches. His name is probably Celtic or maybe Welsh for you have the town of Llangollen there, where Llan *means a church, so it is the church of Gollen or maybe Collen. Certainly there was a Saint Collen who was the Abbot of Glastonbury for some time. I read somewhere that there might also be a connection with pagan fire gods because* Colan *is also Cornish for coal. His festival day is in May and this is the time of year when there is the pagan Celtic fire festival of Beltane.*

Walk on past the church, round the corner and then later on where the road turns sharply left go down the track ahead of you. A stile will take you into pleasant woodland where you keep right at a fork. After a bridge and possibly a wet area walk uphill to your right until you reach a lane that goes to a farm. You will see some trees on the top of the hill.

You will have caught glimpses of Porth Reservoir to your left. It was built in 1960 to supply water to Newquay with its ever increasing tourist population. The end of the reservoir where the small stream goes in, which you will have crossed on a bridge, is a nature reserve and you may be lucky to see many water fowl, especially ducks, moorhens, coots and waders. In the woods to your right through which the small stream mentioned above flows, they used to mine ochre.

Turn right along the farm lane until you come to a gate where you turn right down to Tregoose. *A reminder please to shut any gates that you might have gone through on this walk.*

Downhill now to the bridge, over that stream again, near what was an old mill. *There had been a mill here since the 1560s and I gather the ancient waterwheel was taken away in the war when there was a dire shortage of scrap iron.*

Uphill now to the T-junction where you go right towards Colan but at Bosoughan turn left and back to Mountjoy.

I prefer walks that do not go on roads but this walk along peaceful country lanes is well worthwhile and you can get some marvellous views out to Newquay and the coast as well as visiting pleasant woods and the various points of interest I have mentioned.

17. WEST PENTIRE. PENTIRE POINT WEST. PORTH JOKE. KELSEY HEAD. HOLYWELL BEACH. HOLYWELL. TREAGO MILL.

Distance:	Medium 4$^{1/2}$ miles / 7$^{1/4}$kms
Difficulty:	Easy
Maps:	Landranger 200; Pathfinder SW 75
Start:	The car park in West Pentire village, Map Ref. SW 776606.

You are very close to Newquay here and the lanes and roads can be very busy in the holiday season. You also have a marvellous selection of sandy beaches if it's too hot for walking!

Set off from the car park and turn left and you will see a gate with a sign that tells you that this is the way to West Pentire Head. Don't branch left down to Porth Joke - you'll be there later on. Follow the Coastal Path above Crantock Beach. *Across on the far north side of the beach you can probably make out the silted-up mouth of the River Gannel which flows along the south side of Newquay. In the old days, before the silt clogged up the estuary, ships could sail nearly a mile upriver to dock at Newquay. Pilgrims, merchants, even saints would arrive here from Ireland and then walk across Cornwall to catch a boat at Fowey or one of the other south coast ports to sail across to Brittany. This avoided their having to sail round stormy, rocky Land's End.*

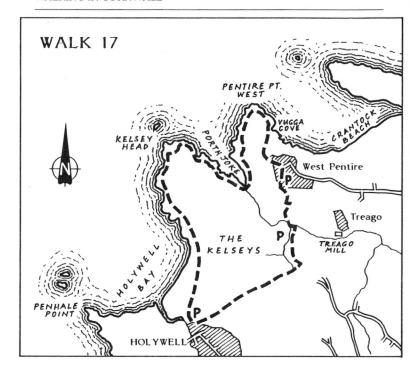

WALK 17

It's a lovely section of cliff up here with gorse and heather in profusion. You will notice Vugga Cove below to the right, a deep gully and a fine place for a swim. The path will take you on now to Pentire West Point and then along the edge of the cliff; watch out as it can be dangerous here in storms. Eventually you will drop down to Porth Joke, or Polly Joke as locals call it. It is a really delightful cove and exactly how everyone dreams a Cornish cove should be. The strange name actually comes from the Cornish word gwic which means a creek, while porth, which you will find a lot along the coasts, means a harbour.

Walk across the top of the cove and once again follow the Coastal Path to Kelsey Head. Like so many of these Cornish headlands Iron Age man built his forts and castles there. You can just make out the banks and ditches of this Iron Age fortification here on Kelsey Head. The *views are tremendous around here as you can look right down the coast as far as St. Ives and up to Trevose Head with its white lighthouse.*

Below is Chick Rock where there are caves in which seals breed and it is magical to sit up here on hot calm summer's days and watch the seals playing in the water or sunning themselves on the warm rocks. You can clamber out to Chick Rock at the bottom of the spring tides but you need great care.

Walk south from Kelsey Head with the mound of a tumulus to your right and a little later on another one. *You will be above a cave that many think is the holy well that is also to be found in the area near Trevornick Farm at Holywell. You will have to walk back along the beach if you want to see it and scramble up into the dark recess, but watch out as it can be very, very slippery.*

You drop down now to the glorious sands of Holywell Beach, a favourite site for surfers who ride the huge Atlantic rollers here. *To the south-west you will be able to make out Gull or Carter's Rocks off Penhale Point, and at low tide a 70-year-old wreck juts gauntly out of the sands nearby.*

At the start of the dunes you must follow the wooden walkboard which is quite a feat of engineering as it twists and turns over the rolling dunes. *The sand here and indeed the whole of The Kelseys is constantly on the move and The National Trust, who own the area, are carrying out extensive planting of marram grass to try to halt the moving, shifting sands.*

Another local legend tells of an old city buried beneath the sands or sea somewhere off this coast. Echoes of Arthur again, with his city of Lyonesse "full forty fathoms deep".

The little village of Holywell (and you will see the well marked on your maps to the east of the main street) offers a chance to stop at the pub to have a snack. Indeed you could also start from here if you wished as there are two car parks.

If you don't stop or when you are ready to go on, turn off left in front of a line of bungalows just before you reach the shop and car park. Follow a sandy path that wanders through the dunes again, past a golf course. A gate will take you onto The Kelseys, a huge area of sand and short coarse turf. *In this delicate eco-system you will see a mass of special plants and wild flowers such as the blue sea holly and other wildlife associated with sand-dunes.* After the golf course there is a gate on your right which you go through and then turn left to follow a wire fence until it also goes left where you go on towards a track. *You are on the edge of Cubert Common, associated with a little village to the south that has, rather unusually for Cornwall, a church with a spire. Apparently John Wesley used to come to this area, probably preaching in the little churches and chapels, as he stayed at a farm called Cairnes just north of Cubert.*

Follow now the track to the bottom of the valley and where it turns right climb over the stile on your left and walk along the wall. After the stream turn left again and walk steeply uphill back to your car.

18. ST. MAWES. ALONG CARRICK ROADS ON THE FAL. ST. JUST POOL. ST. JUST IN ROSELAND. WINDMILL HILL.

Distance: Medium 6 miles/9³/₄kms
Difficulty: Easy
Maps: Landranger 204; Pathfinder SW 83
Start: There is a car park on the quay at St. Mawes, Map Ref. SW 848331. There are other places to park as well. If you are staying on the other side of the River Fal then you could come across to St. Mawes by the ferry, a very worthwhile trip.

St. Mawes is a delightful small town where a great many families with children come for their sailing, beach and walking holidays. The houses rise up in terraces from the harbour, some of them ancient and picturesque. It was a former Parliamentary borough. St. Mawes or St. Maudite, even St. Maclovious, was yet another Welsh saint who ended up in Cornwall and then went on to Brittany. However he lived here as a hermit and carved a chair in the rock for himself above his holy well which used to be near the Victory Inn. However records say that it was probably 15th century having been restored just before the 1939 war.

Set off west along the coastal road by the harbour towards St. Mawes Castle. Leave the road where it turns uphill to the right and follow the track past a car park and you'll see the entrance to the castle to your left. *It's well worth having a look round this castle which,*

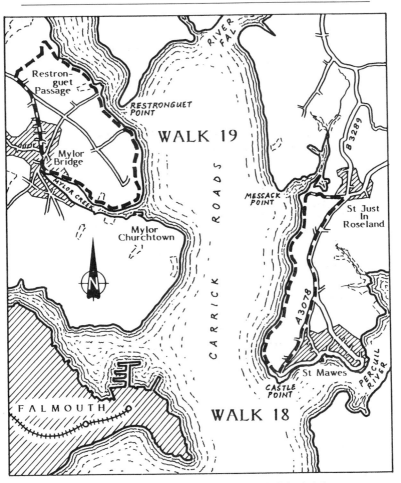

with Pendennis Castle on the other side of the Fal, defended the estuary. They were both built between 1540 and 1543 as part of Henry VIII's coastal defences and with Pendennis were really only artillery forts with huge cannons used to keep intruders out of Carrick Roads. There are several inscriptions in the castle praising Henry VIII and Edward VI.

St Mawes Castle

After visiting the castle go back to the track and walk towards the estuary. Soon you will see a sign that says 'Private Road. Public Footpath' and you walk along with Carrick Roads to your left until you come to a stile which you must climb over to get onto Newton Cliffs which are owned by the National Trust.

This lovely path that runs along beside the estuary of the River Fal is splendid with the tremendous views over the water to Falmouth, Penryn and Mylor. *You might be lucky to see the oystermen of the Fal dredging for oysters with their historic gaff-rig boats that are still built locally; they dip their gaffs while dredging to slow the boats up. It is a marvellous and romantic sight. Estuary birds from gulls to ducks and waders are there wheeling in the sky with shrill cries or flying in tight formation while others creep about the sand and rock pools looking for food.*

This estuary is a ria or sunken valley that was flooded by the sea in prehistoric times as the land heaved and buckled and sank. Many of the estuaries in Devon and Cornwall were formed in this way.

The path is easy to follow. (Don't take the signposted track to your right that would lead you back to St. Mawes.) You cross four fields and then there are some small woods on your right. (You must not climb a stile to your left at the end of the woods.)

But soon there is a stile to cross and after you take the left-hand path by a sign and walk down past a hedge on your left. Another stile, but then ignore the next stile on your left in the corner. By the gate climb this stile. After several more stiles you will come to a footbridge.

Continue on, always with the Fal to your left, crossing stiles until you move inland where at the end of the field there is a final stile by a bungalow. Turn left and this will lead you to a lane. Walk to the right and then fork right. This brings you to the church of St. Just in Roseland which you most certainly must not miss.

This part of Cornwall called Roseland is a magical, secret, still happily unspoilt area bounded on the north and west by the Fal from Ruan and going south to the peninsula at Zoze or Zone Point. Although many of the charming little houses and cottages have roses growing in their gardens the name does not come from roses at all. It comes from Rosinis *meaning moorland island, for Roseland is indeed almost an island.*

The church, another Cornish church right by the water, was built in 1261 but has a 15th century tower. It has three bells, the oldest being the tenor which was first hung in 1684 and has on it the names of two of the church wardens of that time, a small figure of Charles II and two copper coins of that reign. Like so many Cornish churches this is the site of a much earlier church founded by Celtic missionaries as early as AD 550. There is much to see inside. The windows are interesting as are the carved bench ends, a 15th century font and ewer. The roof carving is very fine, while there is an excellent example of a double piscina, a basin and drain where the water used for washing the sacred vessels was tipped. The Victorian tiles were taken up and replaced with good Cornish stone. A brass of one of the early priests completes the list of things to look out for inside the church.

However it is the exceptionally lovely churchyard that is the joy of this particular church and people flock here in their thousands to see it. There are sub-tropical plants that abound in the warm climate of the Cornish south coast here and elsewhere, a blaze of rich colours in the spring and summer. Flowering shrubs and dense overhanging trees give an almost tropical, rain forest feel to this beautiful spot clinging to the steep wooded hill sweeping down to the water. There are two lych-gates, one of which is right down by the water's edge and the other on the road above the church.

It is from this one, perhaps, that you get the best view with the church lying on the edge of the little, almost enclosed creek, surrounded by thick foliage, while beyond glint the waters of St. Just Pool and the rest of the estuary of the lovely River Fal. Aim to get here at high water if you can.

St. Just Pool was once the quarantine station for Falmouth, and vessels from foreign parts, flying their yellow duster, had to anchor here until passed as clean and free from disease and plague! I also heard that there was a scheme to build huge docks here for ocean liners for there are 14 fathoms of water just off the land. In 1919 all the powers needed were passed by Parliament, and plans were drawn up for a new railway line from Grampound Road, dry docks and warehouses. Thank goodness the whole scheme collapsed because of financial difficulties. Can you imagine how this idyllic spot would have been spoilt by such a project?

After the church, walk on down to the pleasant little village and then turn right to return carefully along the road to St. Mawes. *On the whole this is not too busy a country road and being quite high does give some splendid views over the estuary of the River Fal.* You could, of course, if you wish walk back the way you came to keep off the road.

19. MYLOR BRIDGE. GREATWOOD QUAY. WIER POINT. RESTRONGUET PASSAGE. HALWYN.

Distance: Medium 4¹/₂ miles / 7¹/₄kms
Difficulty: Easy
Maps: (See Map P91) Landranger 204; Pathfinder SW 83
Start: There is a car park near the bridge at Mylor Bridge, Map Ref. SW 804363.

This walk is on the opposite side of the River Fal to the one in Walk 18 and will give the most marvellous views across to St. Just in Roseland but also take you along two of the many creeks that make up the Fal estuary or ria. These creeks make for really sheltered moorings for yachts and boats of all shapes and sizes. No wonder this is one of the best sailing areas in the west country if not Britain.

Set off along Trevellan Road and you will see signposts for Greatwood and Restronguet. At a bend in the road you will come across a path that takes you straight ahead in front of some houses.

After going left up a narrow alley, the road ends and you must turn right to reach a gate into a field.

There follows a delightful walk along Mylor Creek through fields, past a quarry and a small wood and a causeway. Soon the path swings north and you come to Greatwood Quay.

The whole of the Fal has traditional links with naval and shipping history and Greatwood Quay is part of that tradition. There was an ancient landing quay here and across the water you will see Mylor Yacht Harbour which was once one of the royal dockyards used by the navy, albeit the smallest in Britain. During the 'packet' service the ships sailing for the Post Office were maintained here until the middle of the 19th century. From here you can look out across the Fal to Roseland and the Carrick Roads.

There should be no problems with route finding as you walk on from Greatwood Quay. By the gates of Greatwood House go right and then left. Signs will lead you on to Restronguet Wier. *This is a favourite walk with local people as well as visitors who come here especially in the spring and summer when the wild flowers are amazing with primroses, bluebells and daffodils as well as many others.*

Both on this walk and Walk 18 I have used the name Carrick Roads several times and you will have seen it on the maps. It is the name given to this particular stretch of the River Fal, 3 miles long and 1¹/2 miles wide. It is the third largest natural sheltered harbour in the world with very deep water in the main channel. You can quite often see huge ocean-going ships anchored here.

After Wier Point you will see Restronguet Point on the other side of Restronguet Creek and the path either leads you across the beach or, at high tide, a permissive path above the beach, until you reach Restronguet Passage.

The Pandora Inn will be a welcome sight, I am sure, as it comes at the halfway mark of this walk. *Rostronguet Passage is another historic village. Passage means a crossing place and this was on the route of the old Post Road from Truro to Falmouth. It meant a saving of time as the longer route had to cross the River Carnon at Devoran and then come on through Penryn to Falmouth. They say that there has been a small ferry in the form of a rowing boat from Feock here for at least 500 years.*

Set off north-west on the signed track along the shoreline. You will pass the Yacht Basin, always busy with the bustle of boats being repaired, painted, scrubbed and antifouled, and here you keep right once more along the shore.

After a while you follow the path inland as it climbs up through fields to Halwyn. By the farm go left at the junction and the track leads you to the road.

The last part of this walk is on roads again but they should not be too busy. So turn left, keep right at the junction near Little Tregunwith and walk on down Bells Hill back to your car.

In some ways this is a similar walk to the one in Roseland but with more contact with the creeks of the Fal as well as the boating world, and certainly a contrast to the other coastal walks on the north coast, with their towering cliffs and huge Atlantic breakers.

20. MANACCAN. ST. ANTHONY-IN-MENEAGE. DENNIS HEAD. THE GEW. PONSENCE COVE. HELFORD. FRENCHMAN'S CREEK. KESTLE.

Distance: Short $2^{1}/_{2}$ miles / 4kms (Medium 4 miles / $6^{1}/_{2}$kms)
Difficulty: Moderate
Maps: Landranger 204; Pathfinder, parts of SW 72 & SW 82
Start: You could start at Helford where there is a large car park but the policy is to discourage cars in this extremely pictur-esque village, except for residents. It is better to start at Manaccan, Map Ref. SW 764250, but great care is needed parking here, especially in the busy summer months. Equally you could start at St. Anthony-in-Meneage where there is also a good car park.

There are a great many variations to this walk which means you could spend several days here trying different routes and, as I have said, I hope you will use this book to discover areas that I may not have written about.

The strange word **Meneage** *is the name given to five parishes of this area and it means Land of Monks.* **Manaccan** *is the word for monk in the Cornish language.*

You may well have a job finding Manaccan driving through the maze of deep Cornish lanes but good map reading will suffice. *The*

Rocky Valley near Tintagel (Walk 11)
Photo: W. Unsworth

The church of St Just in Roseland (Walk 18) *(author)*
The slipway of the old lifeboat station on the Lizard, with the Man of War rocks behind (Walk 22) *(author)*

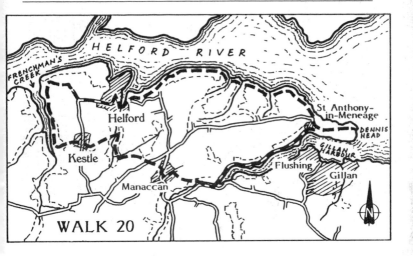

WALK 20

church is worth a visit, not just to have a look at the ancient fig tree, probably about 200 years old, growing out of the wall near the tower. Another church at St. Newlyn East also has a fig tree which bears out the sub-tropical feeling of this warm south coast of Cornwall. There are local dire warnings about harming the trees in any way.

Once again this church was built probably on the site of a cell of an old Celtic monk or hermit. The south door is Norman, dating from the 12th century when the main church was built. However a lot of the church was restored in 1890. The new roof is an exact copy of the old one with some of the original wood for the pulpit, the altar rails and two lovely chairs at the east end.

There is a very odd connection between the village of Manaccan and the infamous Captain Bligh of the Bounty. Apparently he was down in the Helford area carrying out some surveying work for the Admiralty during the Napoleonic Wars. Seeing this figure skulking about by the river the local constable thought that he was a French spy and arrested him! He was then marched in to see the local magistrate who was Richard Polwhele, the Vicar of Manaccan, a well-known antiquarian. Unfortunately Polwhele was taking tea at the time so he told the constable to lock the prisoner up in the cells, which are now the vicarage coal cellar! When he had finished his tea he sent for Bligh who refused to say anything until everyone had left the

Gillan Creek

room except the vicar. Bligh then told Polwhele who he was and what he was doing in Helford, much to their amusement. Bligh and Polwhele became good friends and spent a pleasant evening chatting and exchanged letters for many more years.

Another point of interest is that a William Gregor found near the village a type of rock which he called Manaccanite, which is now known as Titanium.

One final point: the New Inn pub is worth a visit, though you'd better wait until you have done the walk!

Set off down the lane to the east side of the church by the vicarage and you will come to a footpath signposted 'Carne' which you take. It will lead you downhill until you come to some woods. You must then take the right-hand path at a fork and in spring this is a mass of wild flowers. A stream comes down from your right and you will find the road. Walk on left to the head of Gillan Creek but you don't go on to Carne; instead take the road that runs along the creek to St. Anthony-in-Meneage. It is possible to walk along the beach at low water to avoid pounding the road.

Here you will discover another Cornish church almost on the beach.

The story has it that it was built just after the Norman Conquest as a thanksgiving for the lives of some Norman noblemen who were saved when their ship found shelter in Gillan Creek after nearly being driven onto the savage rocky coast in a storm.

There are, in fact, not many Norman remains here but there is an Early English window in the chancel and some Perpendicular architecture. There is a 13th century font and another holy water vessel. Lighting is charmingly provided by candles, like the church near Tintagel.

On the other side of the creek is Gillan Harbour, once a busy port in medieval times when local tin and slate were taken away from here.

After the church you go through the gate into the Bosahan Estate. If you have a dog with you I am afraid that you will have to follow the road back past Tendera and Condurrow and then north to Treath, as they are not allowed here. Otherwise walk on now to Dennis Head. Here you will find not only an Iron Age earthworks (they certainly knew where to build them) but also a square Royalist fortification with gun emplacements. *The Royalists built it in the Civil War to protect the ships in the River Helford. However it fell on March 17, 1646 to the Parliamentarians. The contemporary records state, "S. Dennis Fort, at Helford with 26 pieces of ordnance, is surrendered. It is a place of consequence, and will conduce much to the blocking up Pendennis Castle."*

The route which follows the Coastal Path now takes you back first north and then west to follow the small cliffs and rocks of The Gew and Ponsence Cove and then a small slipway and down to Treath, a pretty little collection of houses. Just before the hamlet you will have come to the road which you follow with a right turn almost to the shore where you must take care not to miss a narrow track that ducks off behind Treath Cottage. In other words do not follow the main road to Helford.

Helford is another of those marvellous Cornish villages with an excellent pub, the Shipwright's Arms, and this name sums up the whole area. With the Fal, this is one of Britain's most popular sailing haunts and you will find many yachts anchored here, especially from Brittany from where those seafaring Bretons come in their small boats in all weathers. If cream teas are what you are after you will find them in Helford.

Across the water is Porth Navas, the home of the Helford oysters as well as mussels and clams. It is no wonder the French sail here with their love of seafood. Upriver is Gweek which like Gillan Harbour was an important medieval port exporting tin. Again as you might expect with all the many little creeks, coves and inlets this was an infamous region for pirates as well as smugglers.

As you drop down to Helford you join the road past the large car park and a little chapel with the supports of the front porch made to look like the trunks of trees.

At the bottom of the hill cross the head of the creek by a wooden bridge and set off down the other side; you'll see the Shipwright's Arms right on the creek's edge in the distance. *There are a number of attractive houses here and further on near the pub many thatched roofs, including the pub itself.*

By a house on your right that is covered with wooden tiles you will see a steeply sloping concrete lane going up to your left; it looks a little like a private drive but it is the way to go. Climb up to the bend at the top and it then swings back left in a hairpin bend. Keep climbing on past houses. At the top the lane begins to flatten out. After a while you reach a road where you turn right and walk down to the gate where you will see National Trust signs telling you that this is a permissive path through the land they own. Over the cattle grid and immediately you are confronted with huge wide-open skies. *Ahead and to your right is a line of pine trees and a lovely glimpse to the River Helford.*

Soon there is another gate and a huge vista looking up the river. *There is a seat tucked in to your right, put there in memory of Peter William Chambers, where you can have a rest and take in the marvellous view.* Here follow the left-hand track until you reach a white gate by a buddleia hedge. The drive ahead here is private and our path goes left through a kissing gate.

The path goes along above Frenchman's Creek through the woods, begins to descend, and then goes more steeply down some steps until you reach a magnificent oak tree. You go left here over a little wooden bridge but you could go right for a short while if you wanted to reach the mouth of the creek.

The woods are dense here with oaks, ferns and mosses almost like a tropical rain forest rising steeply up the slope above you. You might almost expect to see parrots darting in and out of the thick canopy in summer. For a while the path runs through an open area of bracken, heather and gorse before plunging into the woods again until you reach the head of Frenchman's Creek.

Many people know the name Frenchman's Creek from the novel by Daphne du Maurier which was published in 1941. But nobody is quite sure how the creek got its name. It has been suggested that it could come from Frenchman meaning a French ship, as in man-of-war. I gather that Frenchmen was a word used for French ships as early as 1473.

Whatever the meaning it is a lovely place with fallen trees and roots sticking out of the mud at low tide almost like mangrove swamps. Herons hunt here and there are several heronries on the River Helford. You might also see kingfishers, various ducks, cormorants and when I was last here I heard that lovely evocative bubbling call of the curlew.

At the head of the creek the path turns up left to climb quickly to a concrete lane where you continue on up to the left. It soon flattens out at the top by two gates near some ruined barns with yellow arrows to show you the way to the right. The route goes along the edge of the field to reach the road by the farm and group of buildings called Kestle.

Cross the road and walk through the farmyard ahead; make sure your dog doesn't chase the chickens! The fine farmhouse is to your left with a palm tree in the garden. On now through a metal gate into the field. Keep straight along the hedge on your left until you drop down to a Cornish stile with three slabs across forming the barrier on the edge of the woods.

Walk on down through the woods to another Cornish stile by a stream. As you climb a little way up, you come to a T-junction where you turn right. *Again these are lovely woods, mainly of beech with the grey-green trunks soaring up like columns in a cathedral. Quite clearly this is an ancient way as the track is sunk deeply down between banks and carpeted in thick beech leaves that rustle as you walk.*

This ancient track leads you now to the edge of the woods where it swings left at the top of some fields. Here you have a choice. **Either** follow the right of way along the edge of the field straight ahead of you until you reach the road where you turn left and walk to the final right of way on your right to cross the field back to Manaccan. **Or** follow the right of way east along the edge of the wood before swinging right, again to reach the road but here you cross straight over to get onto the public footpath mentioned above that takes you back to Manaccan and your car - and of course the New Inn and maybe the ghost of Captain Bligh.

21. GWEEK. GWEEK DOWNS. POLLARD MILL. PEMBOD. POLLARD FARM. BOSKENWYN MANOR. BOSKENWYN DOWNS. TOLVAN CROSS.

Distance: 5 miles/8kms
Difficulty: Easy
Maps: Landranger 203; Pathfinder SW 52/62
Start: Gweek, Map Ref. SW 706268. You can park near the bus stop or other convenient place.

Gweek is a peaceful little village with two bridges surrounded by woods and gently sloping fields. It was once a busy port lying at the head of the tidal estuary of the River Helford, when it took over the trade of Helston whose own river, the Cober, became silted, eventually forming The Loe and Loe Bar. But Gweek suffered the same fate as the Helford, also becoming silted, and a busy trade with big ships finally stopped from here in 1880. Penryn and Falmouth in their turn took over though they could still get small cargo ships up here until the 1930s. The history of trading stretches right back to the early days when Phoenician tin traders came here and the Romans may have sailed their boats up the River Helford as there are the remains of some Roman forts nearby. From the 13th century and into its heyday Gweek had

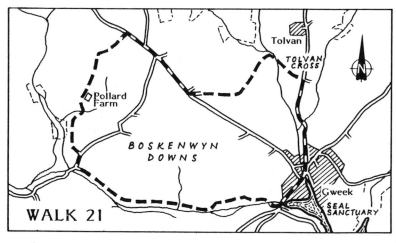

a merchant guild and all the privileges of being a borough. Tin was one of the major exports but it was tin and other mining activities that brought about the final demise of the port for it was the sand, silt and other waste deposits that finally closed the river for large vessels. It still has an attractive waterfront, and is now a busy sailing and boating centre.

As we get further west into Cornwall it is harder to find walks in the countryside rather than the coast, however this walk is completely inland.

Set off on the road towards Helston and cross a bridge. You'll soon come to the head of Gweek Creek where you turn right onto a track by an old mill. You must now cross right over a small bridge on the stream that flows down the valley you'll be following. The track continues past a house on your left and soon you climb a stile. There will be a hedge on your right and later two gates to go through. Fields, woodland and gates are ahead of you but the right of way is easy to follow. Soon you come to a kissing gate.

More fields and a gate before a grassy track leads you eventually to Pollard Mill which has recently been renovated, with the leat still bringing the water down to the wheel, which is also in good condition. *What a shame it is that we still cannot harness water in this way for other small industries in Britain. It seems so economical and, of course, pollution free.* You now follow the drive of Pollard Mill to the road where if you just go left for a few yards you can have a look at the sluice gate that controls the water that flows down the leat to the mill.

Turn back and walk uphill on the road for a couple of hundred yards until you see the entrance to Pollard Farm on your left. Cross the cattle grid and follow the track up to the farm. To your left you will see a view over a very beautiful wooded valley. Drop down a bit to cross a bridge over a small stream and then on to the farm. The right of way goes through the farmyard but fork left to keep the house and a barn on your right. Cross gates, stiles and fields and with the hedge on your left you'll come to Boskenwyn Manor.

You probably will have heard and seen quite a bit of air activity, particularly when you got to the corner near Pembod, as you are almost on the edge of the Royal Naval Air Base at Culdrose. As well as training helicopter pilots here they carry out extraordinarily brave rescues from stricken ships, fishing boats and yachts, sometimes in quite appalling and terrifying storms. Many an injured climber has also been plucked to safety from the sea cliffs by the Culdrose helicopters.

Another extremely modern sight you can't fail to notice are the huge dishes and aerials of the Goonhilly Satellite Earth Station away to the south.

It was 11 July 1962 when we received the first television pictures from America, via the Telstar satellite and the original 1100 ton aerial here at Goonhilly. There are now ten aerials here, one of which has a diameter of almost 100ft.

Follow the drive of the Manor to the road where you turn right. You will pass a school on your left and at the junction, which is the road you were on when you saw the mill leat and sluice, follow the other, left-hand road that leads to Gweek. The entrance to Barton Farm is on your left, as is also Trenowith. After Boskenwyn chapel (good Methodist country here) on your right, take the deep track on your left and follow it down to the stream.

Cross the stream on a stone bridge and walk right and uphill to the road. *You will see the Tol-ven stone in the garden of a house to your left. In Cornish Tol-ven means a Holed Stone; Walk 28 will take you to Men-an-Tol, an even more famous holed stone. There are quite a number of stones like this both here in Cornwall and indeed Dartmoor and as far away as Orkney. They are all said to be able to cure various ailments by climbing or being passed through the hole. There are records here of a child who was ill being passed through the stone nine times! If the ill person then went on to sleep on a mound nearby with a sixpence under his head this would finally bring about the cure. More likely to bring on pneumonia, I should have thought.*

All that remains is to walk back down to Gweek and your car.

However there is one place that you should not miss before you leave, and that is the Seal Sanctuary. You may well have seen the wild seals when on some of the walks. A visit here will give you a chance to find out more about these lovely creatures and see them close-to. You can also discover something of the work of this hospital for sick, injured seals and their abandoned pups, which was started by a miner, Ken Jones, on his retirement. The story of setting up the sanctuary and the work there is told in his book Seal Doctor. *There are a great many things to see as well as an audio-visual display. It is situated on the peninsula south of Gweek where the River Helford widens out.*

22. LIZARD POINT. PISTOL MEADOW. PENTREATH BEACH. KYNANCE COVE. LIZARD DOWNS. GROCHALL FARM. GRADE CHURCH. CADGWITH. DEVIL'S FRYING PAN. CHURCH COVE. BASS POINT. PEN OLVER. LION'S DEN.

Distance:	Long 8³/₄ miles / 14kms
Difficulty:	Moderate to Hard
Maps:	Landranger 203/204; Pathfinder SW 61/71
Start:	There are two car parks you can use, one at Map Ref. 701115 south of the village of Lizard and the other near the lighthouse at Ref. 702116.

The whole Lizard area is very interesting geologically, which in turn gives rise to an unusual plant life in the thin soils rich in magnesium. There is one actually called the Lizard Plant which is mesembryanthemum with red flowers. The exotic Hottentot Fig is found with other salt-resistant plants and shrubs along with the usual tormentils, yellow vetch and milkwort. Naturalists come here not just for the flowers but also the rare insects and of course the breeding colonies of seabirds on the cliffs. It is indeed a naturalists' paradise.

Nobody knows why it is called Lizard except perhaps the serpentine rock could look like the skin of a lizard. I much prefer the Cornish name which is Predannack which means The Headland of Britain, which of course it is. You can't get away from the fact that this is indeed the southernmost point of mainland Britain as every cafe, shop, icecream and house lets you know it. Land's End has a similar problem with everything being the First and Last. In fact Horse Point of St. Agnes in the Scillies is further south! You'll also be unable to move without seeing countless carvings of lighthouses, ashtrays and other souvenirs made from the soft serpentine rock.

Take the Coastal Path by the cafe and descend the steps to Pistil Meadow, as the National Trust sign calls it. However Pistol Meadow is the more correct name. *You will have noticed the many little rocky islets off the coast here, many with intriguing names and the scenes of many terrible shipwrecks. The one with the name Man of War is linked to Pistol Meadow. In 1721 a man of war named Royal Anne was driven onto this rock in a storm and was wrecked. There were only three survivors out of a*

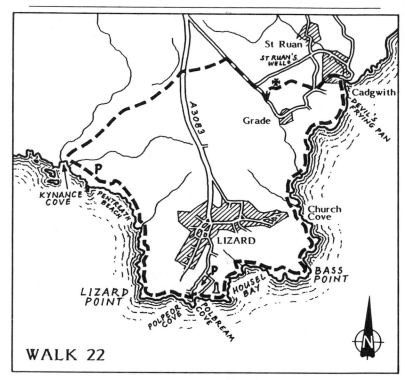

WALK 22

crew of 200 and the drowned were buried here in Pistol Field, possibly with that name because boxes of firearms were washed ashore with the bodies. But more likely the name comes from *pystil* which is the Cornish word for a waterfall. There is a marvellous local story told of another shipwreck that occurred at night. In the morning some of the survivors clambered ashore over the rocks with a pig, which when sold paid for their journey to Falmouth, a barrel or rum that had acted as a liferaft for one man, which was swilled down by the villagers, and the ship's cat which was given to the landlord of the local inn!

Another alien shrub that you will see near the first part of the walk is the Mediterranean tamarisk as you follow the well marked path above Crane Ledges. Steps will take you down to and up from Caerthillian Cove.

Soon you will notice a hideous building in the National Trust car park above Kynance Cove, which contains the loos. From here follow the path down to the cove. *In 1846 Prince Albert came ashore here with the royal children. One way to make sure a place becomes fashionable is for royalty to visit and Kynance Cove has been popular ever since those days. Tennyson also came here (it is a wonder the Arthurian legend doesn't appear here too!) and since then it has also been popular with writers and artists.*

I am sure you will have noticed the many rocks and little island off shore. You may have seen Lion Rock and now off the cove there is Gull Rock, Steeple Rock and the Bishop. But the one to catch your eye on the map must be Asparagus Island that once had wild asparagus growing on it. You will also probably see The Bellows or The Devil's Bellows and this is the name given to the blow-hole on Asparagus Island. At high tides and the right swell it sends great jets of spray into the air with a deep booming sound. At low water you can explore some of the rocks, islands and caves if you have time but take care. Beyond is The Rill and Rill Ledges from where it is said the Armada was first sighted in 1588.

From the cove don't go over the footbridge on the Coastal Path but take the lane beside the stream that zigzags its way towards the car park. Near the top, branch off to take the sandy path across Lizard Downs. Ignore the sign to the left and aim for the houses in the distance.

Ignoring all other tracks keep your eyes on the row of houses on the other side of the moorland and aim for them. *The short heather with light pink flowers here on Lizard Down is Cornish Heath and is unique to this area; the Latin name is* Erica vagans *and is another salt-resistant species.*

The moorland track leads you through an avenue of trees to the road where you will find the houses that have been your goal for so long. Walk down the track on the left-hand side of them. There now follows another section of heathland so take the path that runs across it leaving the track and go towards Grade Church which you can see. *You will also be aware of the Goonhilly aerials - for a few details of them see Walk 21.*

When you reach the road turn right and then bear right at the junction until you come to the lane leading to the church which you follow. *The tower of this little church of the Holy Cross dates from the 14th century and, as you might expect, is made of the local serpentine rock. This is another little Cornish church standing by itself in a remote spot. The story goes that a knight returning from the Crusades was shipwrecked, like so many others, on the Lizard and to give thanks to God for sparing his life he changed the name to Holy Cross. The early Celtic saint was St. Grada from which comes the name Grade Church.*

From the churchyard climb the stile at the east end and walk down by the wall to the left and on to the bottom right corner of a field. A path leads you on to the road. You soon come to a white house and you take the lane to the left of it with another house on the right. There is a sign saying 'South Coast Path (Frying Pan)'. By a farm entrance go left on the lane down to a junction. You can now walk down to Cadgwith which is certainly worthwhile and is more or less halfway round this walk, so maybe a stop and some refreshment is called for!

Cadgwith is what everyone must think of as a typical Cornish fishing village. It is still, thank goodness, completely unspoilt. It lies on the sheltered east side of the Lizard Point and thrived in the days when the huge shoals of pilchards were caught off the coast. You will see the small black building on the north side of the harbour which was the Huer's Hut, Huer being the name given to the lookout who called the boats out when the great shoals of pilchard were seen like a huge silver shadow hundreds of yards long in the clear blue seas. The vast catches were brought ashore and some of the fish were salted down in barrels while the rest were put into the fish cellars where the oil was pressed out for industrial use. The cellars remain but they have been converted now into homes and cafes.

Fishermen still go out from here to put down their crab and lobster pots.

There was a lifeboat here from 1867 and in 1940 the Cadgwith boat sailed to Dunkirk. In 1963 the lifeboat station moved to Kilcobben Cove which you will pass a little later on this walk.

Retrace your steps back from the village and find the Coastal Path past Townplace. *Soon you will see the extraordinary Devil's Frying Pan which is a huge amphitheatre some 200ft deep into which, at high tide, the sea foams and surges through a natural arch. It was formed probably when some ancient sea cave's roof collapsed. The local name is Hugga Driggee; sounds much better than the English one! The trees you passed were unusual dwarf elms.*

The Coastal Path is easy to follow so I need not give details except to point out the great many things of interest to see. *The first perhaps is Studio Golva where you can buy paintings when the studio is open in the summer months.*

You will have noticed here and on other cliff walks the word ogo *which is the Cornish word for cave. As you might expect it is very similar to the welsh word* ogof *with the Celtic roots of language. Here there is Dollar Ogo and Chough's Ogo, a reminder of the bird that is on Cornwall's coat of arms, sadly now extinct in the county. Near here you can see the remains of quarrying where they extracted the black schist with veins of white.*

On now towards Church Cove passing Polbarrow with another natural arch. On the maps you can see Whale Rock and that the cliffs here are called The Chair. There are some stiles to climb that are made out of the serpentine rock. You pass another quarry just before Church Cove. *This is where they took out the serpentine for years and indeed they used rocks from here to build the runway at Culdrose Royal Naval Air base. When crushed it also has many other uses such as making firebricks. Near here you will also see the big diamond-shaped day mark.*

The path drops down into Church Cove. *This was another place where there once was a lifeboat but it was extremely difficult to launch the boat safely so in 1885 it was taken away and the rescues were then from Cadgwith. There is an interesting old fish palace here that has been converted into a private house and an ancient capstan house.*

If you feel like it you might care to wander inland for just over quarter of a mile along the road that leads to Lizard past some thatched cottages to have a look at the most southerly church in Britain. *This is the church of St. Wynwallow (Winwalaus) at Landewednack. The tower with its pinnacles is made, as you might expect, from locally quarried serpentine. There is a Norman door but most of the rest of the church is 14th and 15th century. St. Wynwallow was the abbot of Landevennac in Brittany (more of those travelling saints) and the church at Gunwalloe, here in Cornwall, is also named after him. The last sermon in the Cornish language was given here in 1678.*

Back on the Coastal Path walk on to Kilcobben Cove where you will see the lifeboat station standing in a deep gully. It has been here since 1961. If your knees can take it then you might like to climb down the steps to have a look at the lifeboat. *Both the older boats from the previous stations saved over 1000 lives; 400 for the Cadgwith boat and 600 for the Lizard.*

The fish palace and ancient capstan house at Church Cove

Take the steps down away from the lifeboat station to continue the walk past a strange leaning rock and this will bring you to Bass Point. *Here you will find a coastguard lookout as well as a disused Lloyd's Signal Station built first in 1872, though the present building was put up in 1954. Ships running up the Channel were given visual signals often by flags from shipping agents and insurers about their future movements. Ironically some ships came in too close to see what messages were being given and ran onto the rocks! There is the story also of the German ship* Mosel *that ran into Bass Point at 14 knots in thick fog. The coastguard who heard the bang went down to see what had happened and was able to step directly onto the deck of the stricken vessel! Nearby there is another day mark in the form of a slab of rock painted red and white to help ships avoid Vrogue Rock.*

Near the gully of Polledon is the house where Marconi made some of his early experiments with radio. He was able to send messages from here as far as the Isle of Wight some 180 miles away. There is a plaque here to commemorate this.

Housel Bay has a hotel if you need a final 'fix' to get you back to the start and you can reach it through the gate to your right. You might well need it as there is a steep descent and a gasping climb up steps to reach the point above Bumble Rock (what a lovely name!). *Here you will see the Lion's Den, another huge and jagged hole, like the Devil's Frying Pan, made when the roof of a sea cave collapsed. You may remember Lion Rock at the start of the walk.*

This will bring you to the Lizard Lighthouse. *With the Lizard jutting out into the Channel no wonder there is a need for a light and records show that the first one was put here in the early 1600s and was probably fired by coal. This light was built in 1751 though it was modernised and renovated in 1903, an oil-fired light having been introduced in 1812. Electricity rather surprisingly was first used as early as 1878. The modern light is the most powerful in Britain and has a power of 15 million candles and can be seen, on a clear night, at a distance of 21 miles. There are sinister twin foghorns above the path which you can see and, I hope, not hear when you are too close for they are deafening, head splitting and body stunning. The original ones were built in 1840 but like the light have been modernised to produce a terrible double boom that can be heard 14 miles away. You can have a look round the lighthouse if you wish.*

Nothing now but to get back to your car at either of the two car parks and perhaps have 'the most southerly' cup of tea in Britain.

23. REDRUTH. GRAMBLER FARM. BUSVEAL. GWENNAP PIT. CARN MARTH.

Distance: Medium 4 miles/6^{1}/2kms

Difficulty: Easy

Maps: Landranger 203 and part of 204; Pathfinder Map Ref. SW 54/64 and part of SW 74/84. This is an awkward walk for maps as it just creeps over the boundary from one to another in both Landranger and Pathfinder maps

Start: Redruth. You can park in the town and it is just possible to park carefully at the start of the walk at Map Ref. SW 706419.

Redruth was once the capital and centre of Cornish mining as well as being a charming market town. It has a maze of little lanes and alleys with a wide

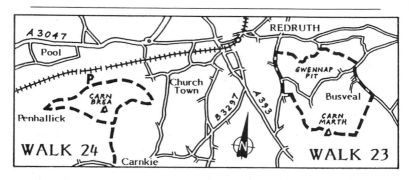

range of different types of architecture from Georgian and Gothic to Victorian. It lies on either side of a deep valley and the name comes from the Cornish for red river. The Scottish inventor William Murdock lived here until his death at the ripe old age of 86. He found that he could extract gas from coal and in 1792 his house was the first in the world to be lit with gas. The railway runs over giant spans of a granite viaduct. The famous Cornish County Rugby Football field is here with its muddy 'hellfire corner' where many a visiting county team has come to grief to the roars of the ever vocal Cornish crowds!

This is one of two walks near Redruth that takes you into the heart of what was once a thriving mining industry; one of the oldest and most famous in Britain. An industry that stretched back thousands of years and is sadly no more.

Cross Sandy Lane and look out for the signposted path that will lead you past Grambler Farm on your left. The track has hedges and you pass an open area to your right. The hedge on your left will take you on to an enclosed track. You will see a couple of gates with a signpost by the second where you turn left along another track.

There is a gap in the wall to your right and you go through this. After the gap turn right and walk along the wall on your left. There is a stile beside a gate which you climb and now walk along a hedge on your left. Another gap will take you into a field which you cross to another stile by a gate. Cross over that and then go past a house on the right and follow the track with a hedge to the junction.

You soon see a lane which has a sign leading you to Gwennap Pit. You will walk past a chapel to reach this extraordinary place which is one of the main reasons for this walk.

Gwennap Pit

Gwennap Pit was probably an old mine working whose roof collapsed forming this natural amphitheatre which the miners converted into a place where several thousand people could meet. John Wesley who founded Methodism came here first in 1762 to preach and he felt that this was such an incredible and yet suitable place that he came back over 17 times until his last sermon here in 1789; he died in 1791. Methodists still come here in their hundreds for their Whit Monday service and to have a look round the memorial chapel. In the mining village of Carharrack there is a small museum of Cornish Methodism in the church which still has its original box-pews and gaslights - William Murdock's invention. The Pit is known as the Cathedral of Methodism and the farm whose entrance you will pass later on is called Cathedral Farm. Methodism and its history is such an important part of Cornish life with its chapels and choirs that it is a splendid opportunity to come to such an important place for all Methodists.

To carry on with the walk, go back to the lane and past the entrance to Cathedral Farm on your right. Ignore a track to your left and then turn right on the track that climbs uphill through brambles. Keep straight on at two crosstracks. There is a ruined cottage on your left and at the third crosstracks you must turn right. The climb continues past a small lake. You might just make out a well to your right but it is well hidden in gorse and heather. Don't go through the gate on your right but keep on to the cement Trig Point on Carn Marth at 235m.

The view is fine, looking out over the remains of the sad derelict remains of the Cornish mining industry. You'll see Carn Brea to the west where the next walk will take you. Look north-east and you can make out St. Agnes Beacon (Walk 25).

If you can drag yourself away from the view, drop down north-west by the fence that protects a quarry and then down a walled track. At the lane that you reach turn left. At a T-junction go left and then right at the next junction back to your car or into Redruth itself.

24. CARNKIE. CARN BREA.

Distance:	Short 2$^{1}/_{4}$ miles / 3$^{1}/_{2}$kms
Difficulty:	Easy but a few climbs
Maps:	(See Map P112) Landranger 203; Pathfinder SW 74/84

Start: You can park carefully in the village of Carnkie, Map Ref. SW 686399 but you could drive on up the lane to the north towards Carn Brea where once again it is possible to park with care so as not to block other people and gates. Map Ref. SW 685406.

This is an extraordinary walk in that it is moorland right in the middle of an urban complex with Redruth and Camborne literally at your feet with, as in Walk 23, all the gaunt ruins of the dead Cornish mining industry around you.

Set off north up the track onto the bracken-covered hill but before you have a look at the castle you might like to wander up left to the 90ft Dunstanville Monument. *It was built in 1837 as a memorial to a local mine-owner called Francis Bassett. You are some 828ft/225m high here and below you lie Camborne to your left and Redruth to your right. To the east of the monument you might look for a large rock that has some hollows scooped out in it by natural water erosion. There are fanciful tales told that these were for holding the blood of sacrifices carried out by Druids; not true as you might expect! It is also known as the Giant's Cups and Saucers. More of that later.*

Go back along the ridge to the castle. *It stands in a most dramatic and imposing site perched on great granite rocks. There has been a castle here at least from the 15th century and certainly since Elizabethan times and was probably used as a hunting lodge, for the northern slopes of Carn Brea were once densely wooded.*

Walk on past the castle and by a leaning slab of rock look for the small path to your right that goes off down the hill towards Carn Brea village. *The whole area of Carn Brea is an archaeologist's paradise from pre-history to the industrial times of the last century. A great many flint arrowheads have been found during the various digs that have taken place here and it has been discovered that Neolithic man lived on the slopes to your right over 5000 years ago. Huge ramparts were built round the summits of Carn Brea by these early men which were strengthened and enlarged by the Iron Age people. It is probable that over 150 Neolithic settlers would have lived in thatched huts on these slopes.*

You will see the church tower and cemetery in the hamlet called Church Town ahead of you as you walk down steeply. At the bottom you come to a track where you turn left. Follow this track until you reach the junction with another track coming in from your right. Go left and where there are some flat rocks on the left-hand side of the track, turn in to the left halfway along the rocks to take the path that climbs uphill towards the ridge with the castle and the monument on it.

You will now be near House of Water, a small pond which is also known as the Giant's Well. For local people Carn Brea was always the haunt of giants and many of the strangely shaped rocks have names associated with giants. There are the Giant's Cups and Saucers, the Giant's Head, the Giant's Hand, the Giant's Cradle and the Giant's Couch.

The dreaded giant Bolster, who probably lived here, was able to stride from St. Agnes Beacon to Carn Brea, about 6 miles, in one huge step! It is said that he fell in love with St. Agnes, who being fed up with his advances, put him to task by telling him to fill a huge hole in the cliffs with his blood. The love-sick giant did as she had asked by cutting a vein but as he did not know that the bottom of the hole was linked to the sea by a cave he bled to death!

Carn Brea Castle

Halfway up the steep hill turn right when you meet the track coming down from the top of the ridge from the castle. *As you walk down you will see more and more evidence of the tin mining and processing activities of the past with many mounds and hollows. There is a disused mine to your left.*

At the bottom go left and skirt round the bottom of the hill, always keeping left until you can see a square rock up on the summit of Carn Brea. Soon a short steep climb takes you onto a man-made platform and beyond several paths branch off. Here you turn off left and start the steep climb back up the hill.

You will have seen the old engine house chimney and then a deep gully running off to your right which is the remains of a quarry, as marked on the maps, where they dug out stone for buildings and tracks to be used for the local mines.

You see a stone wall as you climb and you slant across right to get to it. At the top of the ridge at the crosspaths go straight ahead. This will take you eventually to the lane where you either walk up to your car to the left or back down to the village of Carnkie to the right, depending where you left it.

25. CHAPEL PORTH. TUBBY'S HEAD. CARN GOWLA. ST. AGNES BEACON. GOONVREA.

Distance: Medium 3¹/₄ miles / 5kms

Difficulty: Easy to Moderate with some climbing

Maps: Landranger 203; Pathfinder SW 75, SW 54/64,
SW 74/84. Another really awkward walk for Pathfinder maps as
it just enters onto three of them!

Start: The car park at Chapel Porth, Map Ref. SW 697496.

You will find a cafe here in the summer months. It is a pleasant little cove owned by the National Trust. The bathing can be dangerous though if you are tempted to plunge into the surf. There are some caves and natural arches both to the north and south along the coast. It is possible, at low tide, to walk along the sands here to look at the caves and a view from below of the Towan Roath engine house but the path runs near this on the walk. You can also make out in the cliffs the adits and one of the lodes that were worked by nearby mines.

However the tin-mining village of St. Agnes is well worth a visit first. It is surrounded by the chimneys of engine houses from nearby mines with marvellous names such as Wheel Kitty, Wheal Friendly, Blue Hills and so

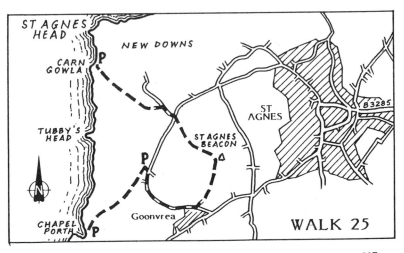

117

on. There is a charming stepped terrace of miners' cottages with the splendid name of Stippy-Stappy. The church has a slender spire, unusual for Cornwall, and rears up above the cottages. Trevaunance Cove lies at the end of the steep-sided combe in which the village stands. Tin ore used to be shipped away from here in the 18th century but the quay built then was washed away by a tremendous storm in 1934. Four other quays which had been built and rebuilt from the 1630s had all been swept away in storms.

To start the walk go out to the north on the Coastal Path from Chapel Porth following the largest track up the little valley. You soon see the mounds that are the only remains of the ruins of the St. Agnes Chapel built in medieval times. *Porth means harbour in Cornish, hence Chapel Porth.*

After a while the track divides and you keep left to arrive at the extremely well-preserved engine house of Towan Roath built in 1872. *This has been restored by the National Trust. The great steam pump in the engine house worked a piston that went down the shaft you can see, now covered with an iron grill, to suck the water out of the Wheal Coates mine. You can make out more ruined buildings of this mine off to your right.* You will be near this on your way back so, if you wish, you can walk over to it now or on your way back, to have a closer look.

Keep on north now on the Coastal Path past another disused shaft. Ignore any side paths. *Be careful as the slopes off to your right are steep and dangerous.* The path climbs uphill and goes left to aim at a bench near a road. If you feel like it you might care to climb on up to St. Agnes Head itself and the disused coastguard station. *From here you can look up the coast to Trevose Head and down to Navax Point near Hayle. Out at sea there are Bawden Rocks or Man and his Man where many seabirds nest such as kittiwakes, guillemots and razorbills.* This little diversion adds about 300 or 400m each way to the walk.

Drop back down to the bench where you turn left if you've been to St. Agnes Head or turn right if you haven't, to follow the right of way inland. Don't take any of the paths to your left. You pass a field with a fence and then join a road.

Once again there is a huge amount of evidence of the industrial past and indeed present, for some of the quarries are still worked. The sands and clays in this area, deposited when the land was below the sea, are geologically very young, only 50 million years old! Off to your left is Doble's Pit where sand has been quarried for hundreds of years. One of the main uses of St.

Agnes sand was for making moulds in smelting works and, of course, in glass making.

Follow this road down to a T-junction where you turn right to reach the main road. Go over by the National Trust sign and walk up the right-hand track to the summit of St. Agnes Beacon at 192m/ 629ft. There is a trig point.

The views from the summit are tremendous, looking out over a large stretch of the Cornish countryside as far as Falmouth and even St. Michael's Mount. Beacon is the name given to a hill where they lit bonfires and St. Agnes Beacon is just that. Fires have always been lit here on special occasions to warn or to celebrate, including I suspect the fires of the Celtic pagan fire festival of Beltane in May. There are cairns up here and it is no wonder that prehistoric man chose this spot to bury his dead.

You now descend the track on the south side of the Beacon. At the bottom turn right and quickly left down a path by a sign warning you of the dangers of mine shafts. At the track go right and then when you reach the main road turn right again and walk on past Goonvrea. Just after the bend, in about 300m, you come to another National Trust sign for Wheal Coates to your left.

Away to your right you can see Beacon Cottage Farm and this is an interesting place. As well as sand being dug out in this area, clay was also very important. There are pits behind this farm where they excavated clay that was used to make waterproof foundations when building piers such as the ones in Penzance harbour. The other splendid use of St. Agnes clay was to hold the candles of the miners on their felt hats or in little crevices in the mine tunnel walls. The famous potter Bernard Leach who lived and worked in St. Ives used clay from St. Agnes for his pots.

Follow the large track having turned left by the sign and then on the second bend take the path leading off left.

If you have not done so already you could walk over to look at the ruined buildings that were the processing works of the Wheal Coates mine. *The whole of this flat area on the top of the cliffs here is a mass of old mines with their ruins and open shafts. Most have been covered with steel grids but great care is needed when walking about in this area of heathland. I often long to be transported back in time, for I would be fascinated to see the countryside here at the height of the mining boom. The air would have been thick with sulphurous smoke and noise and even though nature has taken hold to soften the scars of the spoil heaps and adits the whole area shows what a terrible damage mining industry does to the ecology of the countryside. But now all has been softened and taken back to nature. Ling, tormentil and bell heather thrive on the open heathland.*

Turn left at a bench and follow the path downhill back to Chapel Porth. *This is a fascinating walk with dramatic cliffs and a chance to see at first hand all that remains of the once thriving Cornish industrial past.*

26. NANCLEDRA. TREDORWIN. GUVAL DOWNS. CASTLE-AN-DINAS. TONKINS DOWNS. TRENOWIN DOWNS.

Distance: Medium 4 miles/6$^{1/4}$kms
Difficulty: Easy to Moderate
Maps: Landranger 203; Pathfinder SW 33/43
Start: Nancledra, Map Ref. SW 496360. You will find a car park behind the post office.

This rather scattered village lies on the B3311 from St. Ives to Penzance. I read that it once had three pubs to quench the thirsts of the miners in the days when the local mines and quarries were all working.

This walk takes you into a rather strange, deserted no man's land of old china clay works, moors, spoil tips, Iron Age hill-forts and little tracks and

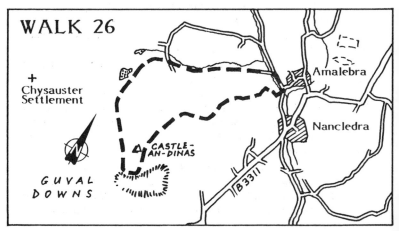

lanes. I discovered it many years ago when I was running a Management Outdoor Development Course here and I often come back to wander around; it's another little bit of secret Cornwall where not many people come.

Start off along the main road and then follow the sign right for Georgia. After a short distance you cross a bridge over the River Red. Later by a house on your left you take the footpath to the left just after it. It's uphill now for a while.

At the cross-tracks climb a stile by the gate on your right. This will take you into fields now with a hedge running on your left. After another stile cross over to a gate by a cottage and the path leads you in front of it and on to another field with a further hedge on your left. *The wild flowers are really marvellous on this first section of the walk if you come here in the spring or summer: foxgloves, wood anemones, spotted orchids, pink purslane and a host more. You may like to bring a good flower guide to help identify them.*

Another stile and the path takes you into a wood and eventually down to a stream where again you will see not only woodland flowers and wildlife but also rhododendrons. Soon ahead you will make out the chimney at Tredorwin. At the junction you must go right and walk behind the chimney.

There were extensive china clay works here in the early 1800s. China clay is decomposed granite and they quarry it still in the granite regions of the south-west, on the edge of Dartmoor and near St. Austell and Bodmin. The maze of little lanes and tracks near here were busy with the carts pulled by horses that were used to haul the clay down to Penzance to be shipped to Liverpool and then by canal to the potteries in Staffordshire. What a journey for Cornish clay.

Walk on and shortly fork left. Once again you will come to another ruin and this time it is an old engine house similar to the ones built near tin mines. *But this was used to power the pumps to keep the water out of the clay pit where they quarried the china clay. There is no pump now so the pit has become a lake with numerous waterfowl on it. By the lake as you continue there are mounds of waste sand left behind after the clay had been extracted.*

After the engine house don't follow the first path to your right but climb over a metal bar through a gap in the bank and continue with a wall on your right. By the waste mound walk through another gap and you will find a path that will lead you to some ruins. When you see two posts go uphill between them with a hedge on your right. The whole area is criss-crossed with tracks and paths. By a wall you find a track which soon divides with the left-hand one, which you take, going to a ruined farm.

After the farm go right along a grassy track. *You are now high on Guval Downs and there are sweeping views down to Mount's Bay and you can make out St. Michael's Mount itself. As you walk on you will see a quarry down to your right.*

Roger's Tower stands out ahead of you if you go through another gap on your left. *It was a folly built in 1798 on a site where there are marvellous views. It wasn't the views that the Iron Age people were thinking about when they built Castle-an-Dinas but a good defensive position. This Iron Age hill-fort lies just beyond the folly. It should not be confused with the better known fort with the same name near St. Columb, which is the largest in Cornwall and the supposed site of King Arthur's castle. This fort here was known sometimes as Endennis.*

Yet another gap beyond the fort takes you onto one of the ancient tracks found all over Britain that were used by local farmers driving their animals to market: the drovers' routes. Once on it turn right and follow it for just over a quarter of a mile to a gate. Here go through a gap on the left and walk on now with the bank to your right. When you get to a track turn left. This part of the walk is now on Trenowin Downs.

Soon turn right through a gate and walk across a field to another gate which you go through to walk across another field to a small gate near the main gate. Two more small gates, both by the main gates, will get you to a lane. Go across it and find a narrow path that takes you down to the road. Finally turn right and walk back down to Nancledra and your car.

27. ZENNOR. TREGERTHEN. WICCA. TREVEAL. RIVER COVE. MUSSEL POINT. WICCA POOL. ZENNOR HEAD. CARN COBBA.

Distance: Medium 5 miles/8kms
Difficulty: Moderate. Some climbs and rocky paths
Maps: Landranger 203; Pathfinder SW 33/43
Start: Zennor, Map Ref. SW 454384. There is a car park here but it may be full at the height of the summer holidays.

There are three things that you might want to look at in or near Zennor before you start the walk or when you get back, unless you are too exhausted by the ups and downs! There is also the Tinners' Arms pub.

The first two places of interest are in the village and one is the remarkable Wayside Cottage Folk Museum. It is an extraordinary and amazingly complete collection of objects, exhibits, maps and photographs from the period of history in Cornwall when tin mining, with all its

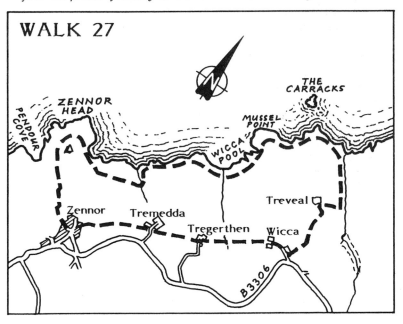

associated industries and occupations, pilchard fishing and farming were in their heyday. It would be useful if you were able to visit this museum before you did any of the walks in this book as it would give you a marvellous insight into the way the Cornish people lived during the last century, including a room furnished in 19th century style with a huge Cornish range.

There is a 10ft waterwheel that came from one of the tin-ore crushing plants in Redruth near the entrance and then a series of rooms and buildings to visit showing you how carpenters, wheelwrights, blacksmiths and shipwrights worked and the tools that they used. One room is an exhibition showing most interesting details of the mining industry of Cornwall. It's most certainly worth a visit.

The next place to visit is the church. A church may have been here from as early as the 7th century though the lovely old church here now dates from the 12th century with many additions in the 15th century. It has the most beautiful barrel-vaulted ceiling. It has been suggested that many Cornish churches had ceilings constructed in this way because they were put up by shipwrights and this is the shape of boats' keels and hulls.

The strange name Zennor probably comes from the Celtic saint Senara to whom the church is dedicated. Apparently there was a beautiful princess called Asenora in Brittany who was married to King Goello. When her jealous step-mother discovered that Asenora was pregnant she was able to convince Goello that the princess had slept with another man. The king was so deeply hurt and angry that he sentenced her to be burnt at the stake. When her executioners found out that she was pregnant they put her into a barrel instead and threw her into the sea. As she floated away over the ocean a son was born in the barrel whom she called Budoc. A good angel kept an eye on them and fed them until they were washed up on the shores of Ireland! Back in Brittany when Goello heard what had happened and realised that he had been terribly mistaken and that the son was indeed his own, he persuaded them to come back to him. On her return journey to Brittany Asenora landed in Cornwall where she founded the church here at Zennor and by now, of course, she was a saint! So the word corruption goes from Asenora to Senara and finally to Zennor. Yet another splendid Cornish saint story.

But I am sorry you cannot start the walk yet as there is another story to come! Many years ago the squire of Zennor, who was also the church warden, had a handsome young son called Matthew Trewhella. Now

The Tinner's Arms, Zennor

Matthew had a fine rich Cornish voice and sang in the church choir. Singing there on Sundays he could not but help notice, being something of a likely lad, that at all the services a most beautiful girl in a long flowing dress would suddenly appear in the congregation. Her voice was also very lovely and soared up into the barrel roof. They must have exchanged glances week after week for they were both obviously fascinated with each other. Then one Sunday, after the service, Matthew followed her out and down to the stream that runs near the village into Pendour Cove. With a faint splash and a ripple on the surface they both disappeared into the water never to be seen again, for the girl was a mermaid. The story doesn't quite end there. One day a fishing boat came into Pendour Cove which as you might expect is also called Mermaid's Cove, and dropped anchor. The skipper who was leaning over the rail was quite taken aback to hear a shout coming from the sea followed by a loud flapping sound on the water. He looked down and saw a mermaid who complained that his anchor had blocked the entrance to the cave under the water where, she told him, she lived with her husband Matthew and their mer-children. And to this day if you go down to the cove on a still summer's night when the sea is glassy calm and gentle swell sends the reflection of the moon shimmering across ripples, you will hear, faintly drifting up from under the water, the two sweet voices of Matthew and his mermaid as they sing a quiet lullaby to their mer-children.

You will also see in the church the Mermaid's Chair which has a carving on the end showing the mermaid carrying a comb and a mirror and her long tail that was covered up with her flowing dress when she came to the services. They have dated the chair to be at least 600 years old, so the legend of the mermaid is as ancient as time. Mermaids appear in many different Cornish legends and are found in the medieval Cornish miracle plays. And if you look at the seat closely it could be that it is slightly damp which means that you have just missed her!

There are many other interesting things to see in and around the church but one that you might care to look for is to be found on the outside wall near the entrance gate. It is a memorial to John Davey. I mentioned earlier that it was Dolly Pentreath from Mousehole, who died in 1777, who was considered to be the last person to speak Cornish as her first language. However John Davey who died in 1891 also spoke Cornish, though probably it was his second language after English, while Dolly spoke only a little English as Cornish was her main tongue. You will also see tombs, some with extraordinary epitaphs, and the granite crosses that marked the Coffin Way, which are found near the grave of Admiral Borlase.

You could spend a lot of time in Zennor Church but it really is time to get on with the walk.

Set off to the left of the church until you see a sign that says 'Farm Area Only'. Turn left along a small lane where there is another sign with 'No Cars, Footpath Only' on it. This will take you to a coastguard building and you need to climb a stile to get onto the Coastal Path. Walk on now north to Zennor Head. *The views from here are tremendous, while all around you are gorse, heather and wild thyme. You might be lucky to see royal fern which is quite common in Cornwall and in the little wet valleys, later on, various wild orchids and bog asphodel thrive. This is all National Trust Land given in December 1953 by A.B. "in memory of friends who have sustained me". The path will take you above Horseback Zawn and a view down on to Pendour Cove and a chance to look for Matthew and his mermaid.*

Don't be tempted to walk up to the trig point at 95m/320ft as you can't get back onto the Coastal Path easily.

After Zennor Head go east on the Coastal Path that drops down towards the shore. From now on the walking is quite strenuous as there are many steep ups and downs with a rocky rough path to follow in and out of granite rocks; ankle-breaking country!

When you get to Tregerthen Cliff you see below you Wicca Pool and the dramatic gully called Cornelias Zawn. *I love this Cornish word for the dark, damp, dank clefts that cut back into the cliffs in Cornwall where the sun, in some of them, never shines.*

Beyond Wicca Pool lies Mussel Point and offshore the rocks known as The Carracks and further on Little Carracks. As you might expect this is another breeding ground for seals who live in the caves here and in the cliffs, often hauling themselves out onto the rocks to lie in the sun.

There is an area on the top of the cliff here that looks like a tended lawn with short cropped grass and, with the wild flowers, almost like a show garden, not a windswept cliff. Walk on past Economy Cove now and along Treveal Cliff to arrive above River Cove. Don't drop down to the footbridge over the river where, by the way, there is a pleasant waterfall but take the obvious track off to the right and inland running up along the side of the valley.

There is a variation here that those of you who feel strong might try. It would add about a mile / 1³/₄kms to the walk. To do this extra section you must cross the footbridge that I mentioned in River Cove and climb on up to the trig point on Carn Naun Point at 97m / 318ft. Go on beyond the Point until you are near the mine shafts where you follow the right of way, to your right, south over fields to some old refuse tips and a disused mine. Turn right here to the head of a track where you go left onto it and then after a short while go right again onto the right of way across fields to Trevail Mill where you will link up with the main walk.

The path that you are following south and uphill along River Cove, if you haven't gone on the variation, is charming with a dense undergrowth of bracken and scrub often covering heaps of stones. There are many wild flowers in spring and summer.

At the concrete track which leads left to Trevail Mill, you turn right past some cottages and then by a house go left and follow the track inland to Boscubben Farm. Just before the main road take the path to the right that will lead you on to Wicca Farm. Here go through the farmyard on the right of way between the house and a barn. A sign 'Zennor' shows you the way. From here the route crosses fields and over granite strips or grids set in the hedges between the fields known as 'Cornish stiles'. You can more or less follow the overhead power cables if you get confused about which way to go.

Soon you reach a small collection of houses called Tregerthen. *It was here, during the First World War, that D.H. Lawrence and his German-born wife Frieda lived for nearly two years with Katherine Mansfield and John Middleton. Like some Cornish to this day, the locals were deeply suspicious of these 'strangers' from up-country, especially as they were 'arty crafty' writers, one of whom spoke with a foreign accent. It is said that Lawrence used to read at night by an oil lamp with the window open and the curtains drawn back. The local people were convinced that they were German spies signalling with this light to a U-boat lying just off the coast by Zennor Head. The situation became so intolerable and miserable that Lawrence and Frieda had to leave.*

Walk on now to the west over the fields that Lawrence would have crossed on his visits to the Tinners' Arms for a drink. Away to your left on the high ground you can see, on the moorland, 'The Eagles Nest' and the old 'Poorhouse'.

The route here across the fields follows an alternative route for what is called the Tinners' Way, which I shall be detailing later, and also the Coffin Way, along which they carried their dead for burial.

The small fields here and on the earlier part of this section of the walk are interesting. Many are quite irregular in shape and date from prehistoric times as far back as the Bronze Age and into the Iron Age, and amazingly they are still being farmed. The whole area around here is rich in prehistoric remains. It's an ancient landscape with old village sites, Iron Age forts, cairns and barrows, standing stones and stone circles. The Wayside Museum has some interesting information and details on these early men and their way of life.

Walk on now until you go to the south of Tremedda Farm. You will soon make out the tower of Zennor Church ahead and work your way back over the fields until you go through a gate between a barn and the church. Turn left to the Tinners' Arms. But if you can bear to wait a little longer, before that well deserved pint, it is worth diverting to walk north up the little track to have a look at the Giant's Rock standing on the edge of some rough ground. *It is an old*

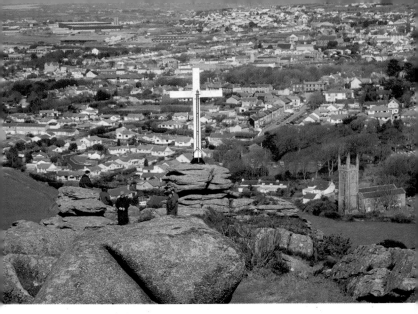

The church at Church Town below Carn Brea (Walk 24) *(author)*
The coast near Zennor (Walk 27) *(W. Unsworth)*

Cist Vean near Chun Castle (Walk 29) *(author)*
Horrace Point where the Logan Rock can be found (Walk 31) *(author)*

Neolithic burial chamber or quoit with a huge capstone standing on seven supporting stones. (There is more information about quoits in Walk 28.) At last back to the Tinners' Arms and keep an eye out for the stone near the pub from which Wesley is supposed to have preached. This is a marvellous walk that I have enjoyed at all times of the year with, once again, wide contrasts of scenery and interest, with a lovely village at the start and finish, full of legends and history that stretches back 4000 years.

28. MEN-AN-TOL. MEN SCRYFA. ROUND BARROW. NINE MAIDENS. DING DONG MINE. LANYON QUOIT.

Distance: Medium 4$^{1}/_{2}$ miles/7$^{1}/_{4}$ kms
Difficulty: Easy
Maps: Landranger 203; Pathfinder 1364 (SW 33/43)
Start: There is a small lay-by, which might be full in the busy season, on the Zennor to Penzance road at Map Ref. SW 419345, where you can park your car. There is a telephone box here too.

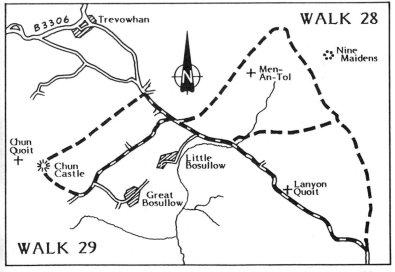

You will see the Men-an-Tol Studio in which was once the Bosullow School. Opposite there is a narrow walled lane that goes north-east. Walk up the lane which is lined with banks of wild flowers of all colours in spring and summer. After a couple of hundred yards there are some ruins on your left and to your right you will see a stone stile and a path across some rough ground that leads you to Men-an-Tol.

Men-an-Tol is perhaps one of Cornwall's most famous prehistoric sites and dates probably from the Bronze Age, making it 4000 years old, or possibly from the Stone Age which would put it at 6000 years old. It is a weird mystical place.

Many learned people including Sir Norman Lockyer, the Victorian scientist and astronomer, have tried to prove that its use was astronomical, marking the sunrise in May and August and the sunset in February and November, which are the Celtic quarter days. However it is more probable that it had, perhaps even still has, a magical significance and function. Men-an-Tol means hole stone in Cornish.

All holed stones are supposed to have healing properties and sick persons are passed naked through this stone nine times at the right phases of the moon, if they are adults. Children are put through only three times but then have to be pulled over grass three times against the sun. All kinds of illness and disease are said to be cured by this method: gall-stones, sciatica, lumbago, tuberculosis, infertility. For pregnant women being passed through the hole gives them an easy childbirth. Engaged couples come and hold hands through the hole to make sure that they have a long and happy marriage with many children. Old women with special powers use brass pins to tell the future by putting them on top of the stone or hanging them on thread. The way they turn, move and point all have a deep mysterious and meaningful significance.

If you feel that you have been cured and can go on, walk back to the lane and continue along it for some 400yds.

You will soon see off to your left, standing in a field, Men Scryfa. Once again the name is Cornish and means Stone of Writing. If you walk over to the standing stone you can just make out, very faintly carved, on the north side, the words "Rialobrani, Cunovali Fili". The word Fili is now actually below ground. These are Latin words but with a Celtic connection and their translation is uncertain. It could mean 'The Royal raven, son of the glorious prince', but there are all kinds of different ways of taking the meaning of the words. If it really is Celtic then it dates from the 5th or 6th century and might have marked a grave after a battle and is also the height (6ft) of the warrior buried here. But equally so it might have been a Bronze Age menhir from 2000 BC that was standing here and had been used by the Celts to carve the inscription after some great battle. Like many standing stones and other ancient monuments Men Scryfa was knocked over or dislodged by treasure seekers digging for gold or precious objects and was known to be lying on its side in the early 19th century. It was put up again in 1824 by a Lieutenant Goldsmith of the Royal Navy. To make sure the menhir did not fall again Goldsmith put it up with at least 3ft under the ground, reducing the height from some 10ft to just over 6ft, so the story about it being the height of the dead warrior can't be right!

Back to the lane again, fork right and go on past a ruined cottage on your left. Soon, at a cross-path, you will see the Four Parish Stone. *Here the parishes of Zennor, Madron, Morvah and Guval meet. This flat stone on your right has a cross carved on the end to make the boundaries; an ancient place where four ancient parishes come together. It also lies on the Tinners' Way, a path which follows an old ridgeway track and of which more details later.*

Walk on half-right up the hill where on the summit you go right past Round Barrow, an ancient burial mound where they discovered cremated remains on a dig. Beyond the edge of the barrow you come to the Nine Maidens Circle. *If you count the stones there are only seven of them, some of which are leaning at an odd angle and others that have fallen or been pushed over and they do not make nine. Dr. Borlase round about the 1750s discovered that there were 13 stones and that there was a single menhir off to the north-west. There could have been as many as 21 or 22 stones originally spaced round a circle of about 25yds. As always nobody is quite sure what the significance of the circle was or why it is now known as the Nine Maidens; no stories here of dancing on the Sabbath or hurling! The barrow has been dated at 1250 BC so this circle may be of the same period.*

Keep on along the track and then aim right towards the old engine house of Ding Dong Mine which I am sure you will have noticed both earlier on the walk and while driving around in the area. *The mine was really known as Greenbarrow but the famous name, known to everyone, may have come from the sound of the church bells at Madron which you can hear from up on the moors. The ancient mine, that*

Lanyon Quoit with Ding Dong Mine in the background

was here long before the engine house, was said to have been visited by Jesus when he came to Britain with his uncle Joseph of Arimathea. The ores from the mine were very rich and its hey-days were in the 1840s until 1878 when it closed because of the discovery of tin in Malaya and the cheap ways of extracting it. In the early days of this century they tried to get Ding Dong working again but it was just not economical. I love standing up here with huge skies and wide panoramas all round to the Lizard, St. Michael's Mount and across to Chun Castle (Walk 29).

A choice now. You can either walk on past Ding Dong and climb over a stile and then along a grassy track to another stile.

This will take you past Bosiliack Barrow, a further burial mound that is probably Bronze Age but could be earlier, from Neolithic times, as excavations indicated and the overall plan of the mound suggests.

From the Barrow continue down the grassy track to the road. Here, if you wish to look at Lanyon Quoit, which I hope you do, then turn left and walk on the road to the entrance to the quoit.

The alternative is to go back to the track that you left to walk up to Ding Dong and then continue south along it. The gravel track soon becomes a lane which you follow until you reach the road from Madron and Penzance after about a mile from Ding Dong.

Here turn right and walk along the road to Lanyon Quoit. Whichever of the two alternatives you take there is some road walking to do but it is certainly worth going to see the quoit.

It is a marvellous example of a Stone Age (Neolithic) long barrow burial chamber, but of course it has been extensively rebuilt and altered over the ages. The Stone Age people buried their dead tribal chieftains in such a tomb, created by hoisting a huge flat capstone to balance on stone uprights. The work and skill involved by these early people is almost beyond belief when you look at the size of the stones. Having created the main tomb they then covered the whole mound in earth and turf to make what we call a barrow. Quoit is the Cornish word for the actual standing stones of the exposed tomb with the earth having been removed - in Wales they are known as dolmens or cromlechs.

Dr. Borlase, who was something of an antiquarian, was also a local doctor and wrote about Lanyon Quoit in 1754 as being so high that a man on horseback could ride underneath the capstone which was then supported by four pillars. But the whole lot collapsed in a fierce storm on 19 October 1815, breaking one of the stone supports. Six thousand years of standing here only to collapse in a gale, but helped no doubt by treasure hunters and even the good Dr. Borlase himself digging about and removing earth from the foundations. Once again local people were so upset that they collected money to have the whole quoit reassembled in 1824 by Lieutenant Goldsmith of Men Scryfa fame. It had lain on the ground for nearly ten years. But it was not as tall nor as authentic as it had been, for Lieutenant Goldsmith, as he had done with Men Scryfa, made sure that it would not collapse again by burying the uprights deeper into the ground and sadly the capstone had been broken in the fall of 1815, as can be seen in the drawings by Dr. Borlase. But for all that it is a spectacular sight with the 13 ton capstone balancing on three pillars.

All that remains now is to go back onto the road and walk up to the right to return to your car. *This is a favourite walk of mine with open heathland, mystical prehistoric remains and as always remains of the Cornish tin industry that you cannot escape, for everywhere you look there are the brittle relics and ghosts of the past.*

29. TREHYLLIS FARM. CHUN CASTLE. CHUN QUOIT. BOSULLOW VILLAGE.

Distance:	3½ miles / 5½ kms
Difficulty:	Easy
Maps:	(See Map P 129) Landranger 203; Pathfinder 1364 SW 33/43
Start:	As for Walk 28, Map Ref. SW 419345

Set off west up the lane, opposite the Men-an-Tol Studio. There is a sign near the telephone box that says 'Chun Castle'. After about ³/₄ mile you will reach Trehyllis Farm.

Go right and look out for a white stone that marks the start of the path the leads up to Chun Castle, through thick bracken in the summer.

Just before the castle follow the track off to the left for about 300yds to have a look at Chun Quoit. *It is a fine example of these Neolithic chamber tombs with a capstone that probably weighs about 8 tons. Cornwall seems fortunate in having so many of these marvellous dolmens or cromlechs, as they are called in Wales.*

If you walk back to the castle now there is much to look at. *As always these defensive hill-forts were built in superbly strategic places and this one is no exception as it looks out over a lot of the ridgeway across which early man walked and traded. It was probably first built in the Bronze Age or possibly earlier but what you can see now has been dated as from the 3rd century BC which is the Iron Age.*

The whole area of the fort has a diameter of nearly 300ft and though vandals, farmers looking for building stone and others have reduced the walls in size there are sections that still stand at over 6ft. It is probable that they are twice that height when first built and there were two walls, an inner and an outer. The south-west entrance is interesting in that you can see that anyone who broke through the outer gate would then have to expose himself to attack as he turned left to get to the inner gate.

You will have to scramble around within the fort but you should be able to make out the hut circles where the Iron Age defenders lived. There is also the remains of a well inside the walls on the north side. Archaeologists have found remains of rectangular huts from the 6th century AD where it is

Chun Quoit

possible that early tin and copper miners lived. I always enjoy pottering around these ancient sites.

Set off east from Chun Castle on the path across the hillside that is signed with a yellow arrow. Soon you find a walled lane which you follow. After a while you come to a stile and a gap in the wall on the right. This will lead you to Bosullow village.

It is best to come here in very early spring or winter as bracken makes it difficult to have a really good look at this Celtic village. Most people know about and visit Chysauster as the more famous and accessible example of a village of about 2000 years old. Many more excavations have been carried out at Chysauster but Bosullow village is well worth coming to.

After the village keep walking east along the lane and a path. Climb a stile which leads you onto moorland where you follow the yellow paint splashes on stones. At the end of the open moor get over another stile into a walled lane which leads you to the road where you turn right to get back to your car.

Note that the section from Chun Castle to the lane is on what is called a Permissive Path and is not a right of way, but there should be no problems.

30. LAMORNA. TATER-DU-LIGHTHOUSE. ST. LOY'S COVE. THE MERRY MAIDENS. THE PIPERS. TREGURNOW.

Distance: Medium 6 miles/9¹/₂kms

Difficulty: Easy to Moderate (just)

Maps: Landranger 203; Pathfinder 1368 (SW 32/42)

Start: The car park on the quay at Lamorna Cove, Map Ref. SW 450241. There can be quite a problem with parking here as Lamorna itself and the cove are both very popular so parking down in the cove can be impossible. You might be able to park in the village with luck, but with care please. Better still try to come here in the off-season.

Above the cove are the old quarries and waste tips that are the remains of an industry that sent good quality granite away by sea from the little quay. Before the quay was built horse-drawn waggons took the huge blocks of granite to Newlyn or Penzance for shipment from there. The Cafe Monaco in Piccadilly, London, was built of Lamorna granite. So was the 22ft obelisk for the Great Exhibition of 1851. The 21 ton column was taken away in one piece again by horses and waggons to be shipped from Penzance. What a task.

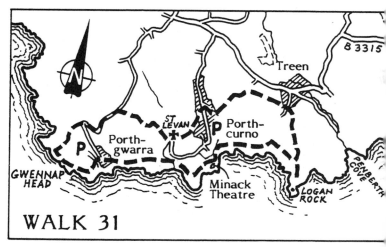

Many artists live or come here to paint and sculpt in these beautiful surroundings and you may catch an exhibition that you can visit. Lamorna means 'valley by the sea' and you will soon be aware of the beauty and light that attracted artists such as Alfred Munnings and Laura Knight to live and work here.

You might also wish to visit the well-known pub called the Lamorna Wink where Munnings lived for a while. The name comes from the fact that it was at one time an illegal beer house that also served smuggled spirits and if you wanted to buy a quick snifter you had to give the landlord a wink!

Set off west on the small road that leads you past the cafes and the quay itself. Soon you will find yourself on the fairly rough Coastal Path as the road and then track peter out; yellow arrows point the way. After a while you come to an old cross standing by a great block of the granite cliff. *I read that there are two stories about the cross. One is that it is the memorial for a little girl called Emma who was drowned with eight other children when a ship, the* Garonne, *was wrecked near here in 1868. The other story is that it was put up in memory of a Cambridge student from Jesus College who slipped and fell down the cliffs at this spot and was killed in 1873. Who knows which is right. But without doubt the drops off to your left are ferocious so be very careful as you walk westwards.*

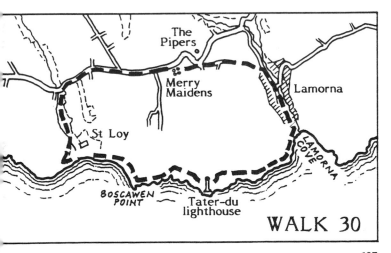

WALK 30

137

The granite cross along the Coastal Path near Lamorna Cove

There is another mermaid story here too but not quite as fanciful as the one at Zennor (Walk 27). A rock offshore is called the Mermaid Rock and a mermaid used to sit on it combing her hair and singing. If you listen carefully you might just be able to hear her even now but don't be lured into the water to try to reach her as you will never come back. It's rather like the legend of the Lorelei on the Rhine who lured sailors to their death by their singing.

Many sections of the route here are a blaze of wild flowers and hawthorn blossom and you will see the little enclosures or bulb fields inland where flowers were once grown commercially to catch an early market, and still there are daffodils and narcissi that have grown wild there. Another Cornish industry that is no more.

The path takes you along Tregurnow Cliff to Carn Barges and ahead you can make out the Tater-du-lighthouse which was built in 1965. *There have always been terrible shipwrecks along here but there was no light on this treacherous rocky coast until the Tater-du was built after a public outcry following the loss of 11 lives from the Spanish ship* Juan Ferrer. *It is fully automatic, like so many of the lights around our coasts nowadays, and can be seen from over 16 miles out at sea. I gather there are some 72 speakers for the foghorn so I shouldn't get too close if it's foggy as the blast is ear-shattering and can be heard for miles along the coast and inland. There is a notice warning you about this.*

Keep on along the Coastal Path until it turns into a lane past a white house. This takes you back again along the cliff to Boscowen Point.

Particularly on the Lizard (Walk 22) you can see lifeboat houses and are aware of the extreme bravery of the RNLI crews. Cornwall is a fishing and maritime county and the crews of the lifeboats, all volunteers, consider it an honour and a privilege to take part in what are often the most dangerous and risky rescues of fellow mariners. It was off Boscowen Point that the whole crew of eight members of the Penlee lifeboat Solomon Browne *made the ultimate sacrifice and gave their lives in attempting to rescue the crew of the* Union Star *that crashed onto the rocks here in 1981.*

After the point it's rough going and then finally downhill to the beach at St. Loy's Cove. *All around there is a feeling of a tropical lush micro-climate for St. Loy is said to be the warmest place in England. Care is needed as you cross the rounded boulders on the beach, especially in rain when they can be very slippery. The cove seems to attract a lot of storm-*

blown flotsam and jetsam that piles up on the beach.

You will see the Coastal Path after crossing the beach where it goes over a small footbridge and climbs uphill. After a drive there are steps that lead you to a fence where our ways divide for the Coastal Path goes left on to the west while you must go right.

Once again a yellow marker on a post will show you the way to go on a narrow path rather than the main track. It takes you round a garden and then climbs up through a lovely wooded valley full of hydrangeas. Two gates now and you will find yourself on the road from Newlyn, the B3315. It is now road walking for a while but there is no other way that you can visit two sites of Cornwall's most famous standing stones.

Turn right along the road until you reach Boskenna Cross. *It is difficult to date the cross but probably it was carved just before or during Norman times. If you have a close look you will see a carving of Christ so it is probable that this was a place of worship on a journey. Apparently it fell down in the dim and distant past and was buried. It was only rediscovered in 1869 when they were widening the road. At first they put it up close to the road junction but it was knocked over so often it was then moved to the lay-by where you see it now.*

If you really don't want to walk on roads and don't mind missing the Merry Maidens and the Pipers then you can go over the stile by the cross and follow the old path used by people going to church at St. Buryan and the rights of way clearly marked on your maps to Boscawen Ros Farm. This takes you close to the menhirs which you will see to your right in the field. On to Tregiffian and Rosemodress. After that you will reach Tregurnow and then back to Lamorna by the route explained at the end of the main walk.

If you decide to keep on the road you pass Tregiffian Barrow to your right. *Like many of these Bronze Age barrows, Tregiffian has been disturbed and looted over the ages by treasure seekers and people wanting stones for building. However archaeologists did find an urn and cremated remains which helped date it. The roof slab looks like a menhir, being fairly narrow, that was put there after the original roof had been removed. On the far side there is an interesting slab of 'rock' that has 25 carvings on it called cup marks. There are 13 circles and 12 oval shapes. It has been suggested that this might have something to do with the full and new moons. If you look closely you will discover that this stone is in fact a replica as the original is in Truro Museum.*

On now to the Pipers and the Merry Maidens. *The Pipers are on private land and are near a farm called Boleigh that may mean 'place of blood' for there was supposed to have been a fearsome battle here when the Cornish under King Howel were defeated by the Saxon Athelstan in the 10th century. However the stones are at least Bronze Age and probably Stone Age and may be connected for religious purposes with the stone circle of the Merry Maidens. The well-known legend goes that these menhirs, the Pipers, come to life at the full moon and the sound of their pipes wafts gently through the night enticing people to dance. One Sunday night, at the full moon 19 naughty young maidens came here from Lamorna and St. Buryan instead of going to church. In the distance they heard the Pipers playing gentle wheedling tunes at first. The girls began to dance and slowly the music got faster and faster and the girls were whirling round and round in a frenzied circle. Suddenly as the music reached fever pitch there was a crack of thunder and a vivid flash of lightning and the maidens were turned to stone. The next day, when the girls did not return home, worried parents came up to the field here to find only the 19 stones; all that remained of their wicked daughters. As they were caught in a moment of high frenzy there are said to be extraordinary powers of energy radiating from the stones.*

From the Merry Maidens cross the field where they are and climb over a stile and then after crossing the field go over another stile back onto the road. It's here that you will see the Pipers to your left. Take the next stile on the right and aim across the field there. There is another stile on the far side which leads you into the lane beside Borah Chapel. Take the lane south-east and you pass near Tregurnow Cross which you can only see by climbing up the bank. *It is very simple; just a slab of granite with a cross carved in it.*

On to Tregurnow itself where you go left down the lane to Lamorna through a gate. Soon you bear sharply left to reach the village. I should practise your winking if I were you! If you can't wink then turn right to get back down to the cove and your car.

141

31. TREEN. LOGAN ROCK. PORTH CURNO. MINACK THEATRE. ST. LEVAN'S WELL. PORTHGWARRA. GWENNAP HEAD. ROSKESTAL. ST. LEVAN. ROSPLETHA. PORTHCURNO. TRENDRENNEN.

Distance:	Medium 6 miles / 10kms
Difficulty:	Easy / Moderate
Maps:	(See Map P136-137) Landranger 203; Pathfinder SW 32 / 42

Start: The car park to the south of the village of Treen, Map Ref. 395229. As with Lamorna there can be acute problems parking at the height of the season.

The delightful village of Treen with its excellent pub is a cul de sac and with the famous Logan Rock about three-quarters of a mile away many people who are not necessarily walkers come here to have a look at it. You could cut into this walk, by the way, from the car parks in Porthcurno or St. Levan and find your way to the Coastal Path which you need to follow for the first part of the walk.

You will find that the pub in Treen, the Logan Rock Inn, gives you information about the Logan Rock and Lieutenant Goldsmith RN (see below).

You start the walk by following the right of way south from Treen that leads you across fields and stiles until you hit the Coastal Path. You will have to come back to it but cross over it and walk past the ramparts of the Iron Age earthworks to your right until you come to the huge towering blocks of granite where you will see the Logan Rock that stands on Horrace Point. *This is a marvellous area of granite slabs and castle-like blocks. With care you can clamber around and look out along the coast both west to Pedn-men-an-mere or east to Merthen and Boscawen Points. Right away to the east on a fine day you will see the Lizard. I remember seeing basking sharks circling round and round in the clear turquoise blue water of Porth Curno Bay on a hot June day with a calm glassy sea.*

Logan means a moving rock and it comes from the Cornish verb log *that means to move. It is 80 tons and you will be hard pushed, literally, to make it move! It used to rock with just the pressure of a finger until young Lieutenant Goldsmith (nephew of the poet Oliver) dislodged it with a band*

*The Logan Rock is the big block balanced to the right
on the nearest rock face.*

of high-spirited fellow sailors from HMS Nimble in April 1824. Perhaps
they had been in the Logan Rock Inn beforehand and were indeed high
spirited! Anyway there was such a row both from local people and visitors
that when word got back to the Admiralty Lieutenant Goldsmith was made
to hoist it back into position with a huge team of men using scaffolding,
pulleys, ropes and lifting gear. It cost him the enormous sum of £130 8s 6d!.

Clamber and walk back to the Coastal Path and follow it west,
keeping inland by old fields along Treen Cliff to Percella Point and
Carn Kizzle. Don't wander off on the lower path here as it can be
dangerous and the drops frightening.

The path runs between hedges and you drop down past a
lookout built during the last war and a daymark for navigation in
the shape of a pyramid. *This also commemorates the laying down in
1880 of the first transatlantic cable to Nova Scotia via Brest. Porthcurno
village, just inland, is well known for its connections with cable and
wireless engineering. Many of the early submarine cables started from here
including one to India in 1870. Cable and Wireless is the company that took
over from The Eastern Telegraph Company. There is a training school here
and a museum. There are also galleries cut deep down into the granite that*

The Minack Theatre near Porth Curno with Horrace Point and the Logan Rock in the background.

were used in the Second World War to protect the vital cables. What a different world to today's satellite communications.

The Coastal Path leads you right back round the head of the cove and crosses over the track coming down from the car park and the village. Soon you have to climb up some very steep rock steps where you must go carefully as you would end up in the sea if you fell!

Climb and then walk on until you come to the Minack Theatre. *You can visit it for a small charge. It was built in the 1930s by Miss Rowena Cade, who used to live nearby, in a natural amphitheatre in the rocks high up on the cliffs. It is a most spectacular site and is said to be like the Greek and Roman theatres found on the cliffs of these Mediterranean countries. As we are in Cornwall there is a Celtic influence, as you might expect, found in some of the designs in the cement that most of the theatre is made from. During the summer, when the weather is fine, amateur dramatic societies come here, especially from universities and youth groups, to put on productions. It can be a most moving and magical experience and is a marvellous setting for the dramas acted with enormous enthusiasm by the young players.*

On now along the Coastal Path and you may want to detour a

little to walk out onto Pedn-men-an-mere for the views.

There are steep climbs in and out of Porth Chapel with its sandy beach hemmed in by sheer granite cliffs. The descent can be dangerous for the not so sure-footed so if you want to go down tread carefully. The bathing here can also be treacherous but it is certainly a secluded and lovely cove.

The path leads you past the Holy Well of St. Levan with its protecting wall and roofless Baptistry in the valley. *The holy water is said to cure eye problems. You can visit the church at St. Levan later on.*

Uphill now and join a track coming in from your right after Carn Barges. The headland of Carn Scathe is off to your left and the rocky path drops down between banks, then you go left at a signpost and right at the next one and finally left by Cove Cottage. The rock tunnel will bring you to the small fishing hamlet of Porthgwarra. *They still haul the boats out by a windlass to get them above the high tides in stormy weather. Again there are high granite cliffs on either side of the cove. Horses and carts used to be driven down to the beach through the tunnel to collect seaweed to put on the fields as fertiliser.*

Keep on the Coastal Path past Hella Point and you can see landmarks again: a red cone and a black and white tower. *These are to warn shipping of the infamous Runnel Stone Reef about a mile out to sea. You might just be able to make out the buoy marking the rock and even hear it for it has a bell that clangs as the swell rocks it.*

You are soon on Gwennap Head, sometimes known as 'The Other Land's End'. *I prefer it to the real Land's End which has become a honey-pot tourist attraction. In fact I have not included any walks near there though it is a marvellous area if you can get away from the masses.*

Gwennap Head is known as Tol-Pedn-Penwith in Cornish which means 'the Headland with a Hole' and there is indeed a cave on the point that has collapsed, giving the headland its name. The huge beetling cliffs around here are magnificent and as you would expect it is a favourite place for rock climbers. There is a Mountain Rescue Post nearby.

The views from here are famous and on a fine day you might just be able to make out the Wolf Rock lighthouse some 8 miles away to the south-west. The wild clifftop flowers are a delight and even the granite rocks have fascinating lichens and mosses growing on them.

By the coastguard lookout on the cliffs turn north-east on the path that leads to the coastguard station. Beyond the station the track crosses a stream and then climbs uphill to a steep bend on the

The tunnels at the fishing hamlet of Porthgwarra.

road that leads to Porthgwarra. Follow the road now to Roskestal.

From here if you want to add a little to the walk you can keep on up the road for just under half a mile until you find a stile on your right that will put you onto a right of way south-east on a well-worn path that crosses several fields and over granite Cornish stiles until you reach an old cross.

Alternatively you will see a right of way off to your right in Roskestal that runs east across fields and a green lane that also leads you to the old granite cross mentioned above.

At the cross join the other route and walking gently downhill across fields, over stiles and through gates south-east, you come to a cottage and arrive opposite the church of St. Levan.

St. Levan, a 6th century Celtic saint, was something of a gentle eccentric who was fond of fishing. Inside the church there is a fine Norman font and some interesting bench ends with carvings that are well worth looking at. There is a jester in cap and bells, two eagles, a shepherd and two fishes on one hook which may refer to the legend of St. Levan.

In the churchyard is an extraordinary stone known as St. Levan's Stone that looks as if it has been split exactly in two by some mighty force. It is said that St. Levan rested here when he became tired of fishing. An old adage says:

> *When with panniers astride,*
> *A pack horse can ride*
> *Through St. Levan's Stone,*
> *The world will be done.*

The rest of your walk runs through fields on rights of way, the first one setting off just north of St. Levan's Church slightly north-east to Rospletha. To the north of the collection of buildings another path goes almost north to Porthcurno village.

The right of way from here climbs very steeply up the hill towards the masts on the top and again across fields to Trendrennen in a northerly direction. Finally north of this group of farm buildings you will find another right of way running west back to Treen over quite a number of fields. *Back in Treen you can regain your strength in the Logan Rock Inn and have a final quick check on the details of Lieutenant Goldsmith's epic hoisting of the Logan Rock back onto its base that led him, possibly in remorse, to set about putting up many other fallen Cornish stones and menhirs.*

Long Walks

I have included only a relatively small number of walks in this book when you consider that Cornwall is nearly 100 miles long from the Tamar to Land's End, but you will be able to find many more by looking at the rights of way on your maps and maybe diverting off some of the walks I have written about to find alternative circuits. The following are brief details of some of the longer walks that you can find in Cornwall that may require your spending a night en route in a bed and breakfast or hotel, especially the first one which runs from the north coast down to the south in central Cornwall, a distance of nearly 30 miles.

The Saints' Way *Forth an Syns in Cornish* is a route that crosses from Padstow to Fowey on the paths and lanes that the Welsh and Irish saints used in the Dark Ages between AD 400 and AD 700, but it probably started as a trading route as early as the Bronze and Iron Ages. To cross Cornwall by land and then on by sea to Brittany and beyond avoided having to battle round the stormy, savage and treacherous waters of Land's End, considered in those days (and maybe still) as the Cape Horn of Britain! But certainly by the Dark Ages it was being used by the Celtic missionaries who were sailing in from Wales and Ireland to convert the Cornish to Christianity and, as you can see from any map, bringing their names to villages, churches, holy wells and ancient granite crosses. Even though it was a journey made in those early times it offers now a marvellous opportunity to grasp Cornish history as the route passes by ancient prehistoric remains and burial chambers from the Bronze and Iron Ages, fine medieval churches and villages from Norman times, to a Cornwall of the last few centuries with mining, quarrying and farming villages with their Wesleyan chapels and rows of terraced houses. It crosses at least 12 parishes and wanders through a most marvellously varied Cornish countryside. The strong walkers amongst you may be tempted to try to walk the whole of the Saint's Way in one go. I hope you won't as you need to look and wonder as you go, so I have divided the whole journey into four sections where you can probably spend the night or come back each day to continue the walk. Or you can break the walk at any point you wish if you can find accommodation nearby. All the Long Walks are linear.

You will find that the Saints' Way is waymarked throughout its length with special and distinctive signs, so routefinding is easy.

32. THE SAINTS' WAY PART 1
PADSTOW. DENNIS HILL. CREDIS CREEK. LITTLE PETHERICK. TRENANCE. BLABLE FARM. WEST PARK FARM. ST. BREOCK DOWNS. TREGUSTICK FARM. WITHIEL.

Distance:	Long 10 miles / 16kms
Difficulty:	Easy
Maps:	Landranger 200
Start:	The church of St. Petroc, Padstow, Map Ref. SW 915715.

By tradition the start of the Saints' Way is from the south door of Padstow's parish church of St. Petroc. It was here that the Welsh saint founded a small monastery in AD 520 and another in Bodmin. He was perhaps the greatest of all the Cornish saints and quite a lot is known about him. He sailed into the Camel estuary in the 6th century and lived for over 30 years at Lanwethinoc. He travelled to Rome on two occasions on pilgrimages. Many legends about him survive; of how he turned water into nectar and also tamed a terrible dragon that was plundering the Cornish countryside. He tied his stole round its neck and took it down to the sea near Padstow from where it swam away and vanished over the horizon never to be seen again! He converted Prince Constantir to Christianity and forced him to spend his life in poverty and prayer in a cell near the bay named after him. The holy relics of St. Petroc were so venerated that in AD 1177 some Augustinian monks stole them and took them to St. Meen in Brittany. It caused such a terrible row that Henry II of England, who was also Overlord of Brittany, ordered that they should be returned. They arrived back first in Dartmouth in a beautifully carved ivory casket which Henry II had given to contain the relics and then found their way back to Cornwall where you can still see the casket in the south wall of Bodmin parish church.

Padstow itself is an attractive medieval town and has many fine houses dating from the 15th century such as Abbey House on the South Quay and Court House which belonged to Sir Walter Raleigh on the North Quay.

Many Cornish miners left from here for America in the last century. It always has been and still is an important fishing centre and of course one of the few inlets in this savage north Cornwall coast.

The well-known great tradition of Padstow is May Day and the leading of the Hobby Horse through the streets to the almost hypnotic music of the May Morning Song. It is quite clearly a pagan festival linked with fertility and other deep Cornish myths and legends. It is said that if a maiden gets drawn in under the black hooped gown of the 'Obby 'Oss she will become pregnant! It is an extraordinary experience to be in Padstow on May Day and to be drawn into the magic of the emotions and frenzy and watch the great 'Oss go prancing and swirling through the streets in a wild dance, with its terrifying mask and flowing mane, the great black skirts and fierce wooden snappers. It is a jealously guarded privilege to carry the 'Oss and to take the part of the 'teaser' who dances in front of the 'Oss with a club. They are members of what are called the 'Obby 'Oss gang. One can sense and, in some respects, become part of the deeply rooted pagan feelings of these Celtic people on May Day.

The church where you start the walk is worth looking round. It was built of local blue-coloured slate from near Harlyn Bay in the 15th century. The carved bench ends are fun with one showing a fox preaching to geese while the pulpit is Elizabethan. There are also some stocks near the font which were last used in 1840 after three drunks fell asleep during the sermon!

Set off through the lych-gate to the south and walk along a wooded path to Hill Street. Go over the crossroads into Dennis Road and then Dennis Lane which leads you down to Dennis Creek. Signs will show you the way to go uphill steeply to the summit of Dennis Hill where you will find the obelisk commemorating the Golden Jubilee of Queen Victoria in 1887. It is a fine viewpoint from here looking back down to Padstow and over the Camel Estuary and away inland to Rough Tor on Bodmin Moor.

Follow the signs down and along Little Petherick Creek and eventually Trerethern Creek. Opposite you can see Sea Mills which was a mill worked by the ebb and flow of the tides. You can cut across the top of a field and then on towards Credis Creek above an area of gorse. The large house inland is a farm called Treravel built in Victorian times but which legend has it was where St. Petroc died on his way to Padstow; there must have been a farmstead here from those early times. Steps lead you

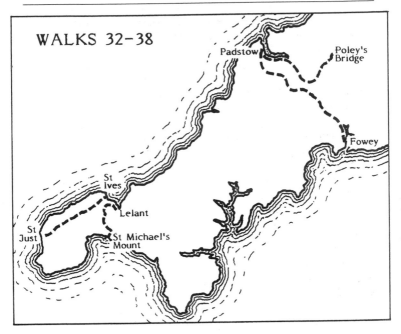

down to Credis Creek itself.

More farms with history and stories. Trevisker Farm became infamous in 1813 for it was here that a young girl set fire 'to a mow of wheat' when corn was in such extremely short supply that the miners revolted. For this she was hanged at Bodmin Goal.

Cross over a footbridge now below Credis Farm. *It was near here that there used to be a mine that exported copper extracted by some 50 miners working over 30 fathoms down (mine depths are given in fathoms).*

Once over Credis Creek aim south across fields, not along the creek itself. Again there are public footpath signs to show you the way down through a little wood. Soon you come to the main A389 road and the village of Little Petherick. *The church here is also dedicated to St. Petroc and is tucked into the hillside. Petroc founded an early cell here near a spring. In a house nearby called St. Mary's lived Athelstan Riley, an antiquarian and a leader of the Anglo-Catholic movement in the early days of this century. He did a lot to restore the charming little church and employed Sir Ninian Comper to carry out this work in the 1890s. There is very fine stained glass and a painted screen. Athelstan actually designed the minute village hall near the bridge in 1907 and wrote St. Petroc's hymn. A versatile man!*

After the village there is a short walk along the main road until you reach a blue slate stile on your right which you climb to enter a field and down to the bottom of the valley to Mellingey; there is an old mill here. Back on a small road again you soon reach Trenance, a small collection of cottages. From here a track runs east and in the valley you will find a slate quarry.

Footbridges take you over a stream, and a path across fields leads you to Blable Farm. After the farmyard you turn right along a lane to reach the busy A39. Cross the road to reach West Park Farm and No Man's Land; what a marvellous name. After a hundred yards or so take the path to the left and uphill through woods until you reach some fields and stiles that have been built specially for the Saints' Way route. Now begins a slow climb onto St. Breock Downs.

It is a great relief for me to get away from the lowlands with its lanes and roads and emerge onto high open country again with huge fields and a massive sky above. Like so many open areas skylarks pour out their distant lovely song and buzzards wheel overhead. Once again the views are splendid, looking out over Wadebridge to the north-east as you walk on to lonely Pawtonsprings Farm. This is sheep country.

You will notice large burial barrows around you and if you look at the map there are many tumuli marked. Soon, as always with areas such as this, you come to the Longstone. We are back now in Bronze Age country and here is another of these mysterious standing stones; it was probably surrounded by a cairn originally. In medieval times it became a meeting place and was called Men Gurta which means Stone of Waiting. On St. Petroc's Day, June 4, each year the priests and people of the parishes of Little Petherick, Padstow and Bodmin would meet for a special service commemorating their patron saint, St. Petroc, the 'father of all Cornish saints'.

Once again the views are outstanding. You can look back the way you have walked to the Camel Estuary and Wadebridge. Further away are the distant skylines of Rough Tor and Brown Willy.

When you reach the road turn left and then the second turning right near St. Breock Downs Farm. From here you begin the descent off the high ground but the views are fine still, especially off to the north-east where you can see the mass of Hustyn Wood. *You are now in the depths of a secret Cornwall that not many people see unless they are walkers or locals.* Road walking now, but not a busy one.

After the road turns south you must leave it and follow a track along the edge of two fields. Over another field and you come to a stony tree-lined track that leads you down to Tregustick Farm. *Ahead you can make out Withiel Church and Helman Tor where the route will pass later, and even Bodmin Beacon with its obelisk.*

After the farm the road takes you down to a ford where if the water is too deep you can cross on the wooden bridges. A steep climb up a lane brings you to the delightful little village of St. Withiel but the church rather surprisingly is dedicated to St. Clement. *This is a long section of the Saints' Way but obviously you can shorten it if you wish.*

33. THE SAINTS' WAY PART 2
WITHIEL. RETIRE. TREMORE. HIGHER WOODLEY. LANIVET. REPERRY CROSS. TREBELL. HELMAN TOR.

Distance:	Medium 7 miles / 11$^{1/}$₂kms
Difficulty:	Easy
Maps:	(See Map P151) Landranger 200
Start:	Withiel, Map Ref. SW 995654.

You might have ended Walk 32 in this delightful little village but sadly there is nowhere to get a meal or stay right in the village itself. Withiel lies in a splendid no man's land of rolling lovely countryside in the middle of nowhere! The medieval church of St. Clement is worth looking at. There is also an old rectory built in the 1520s by Prior Vyvyan who was the last prior of St. Petroc's in Bodmin before the Dissolution of the Monasteries.

From the church take the road south and before the steep hill go over the stile on your left into land of Churchtown Farm. More stiles and fields follow until you drop down to the stream in the valley bottom near Lanzota. *It was probably near here that the original settlement of Withiel was founded by a long-forgotten Celtic saint called Zota or Zawda near the stream. If you look at the maps you will see*

Withielgoose (what a marvellous name) to the east which is a Domesday Manor.

Two more fields and you find yourself in a narrow lane lined with a mass of hedgerow flowers in spring and summer. This will lead you down to Retire, a strange name that comes from the Cornish *Red-hyr* meaning a long ford. *There are several old cottages here and an 18th century meeting-house which is now the chapel schoolroom for there is a Methodist chapel nearby.*

From Retire a track above the hamlet takes you to a stile on your right and then a field. After the gate on the far side there are some very steep steps that lead you on to the road. You now follow this medieval road from Bodmin to St. Columb Major and on to the old clapper bridge of Tremore where the small stream flows north eventually to join the Camel. *South from here there was a lot of mining both for tin and iron.*

After the 18th century Tremore Farm and Cornish Manor (now a Christian Fellowship centre) you arrive at a crossroads with an ancient cross by it and the now familiar Forth an Syns (Saints' Way) marker post. This points to the south where you walk to Higher Woodley and from there cross fields before joining small roads to take you to Lanivet. *Here you come back to reality with a roar and engine fumes after the calm of the depths of the Cornish countryside, for the busy A389 runs through the village. It is not as busy as it used to be because this was the main road for both holiday and local traffic going west on the A30 before 1975 when the Bodmin by-pass was opened.*

Away from the road is a charming village green, a fast-flowing stream and the parish church of St. Nivet. There are several places where you can get a meal or a drink and even stay if you wish to break your journey here. This is the halfway point of the Saints' Way. Both the church and the churchyard are worth wandering round. Inside there is a 15th century font and the remains of a Saxon column. I gather that in 1539 the people of Lanivet were able to buy the four bells from Bodmin Priory, after it had been dissolved, for the huge sum of £36.00! In the churchyard there are two ancient crosses and 10th century gravestones near the south porch and an interesting Hogback tombstone. If you have time and want to walk south for 10 minutes on the A389 you will come to St. Benet's Abbey. It was built in the 15th century and became a Lazar House or hospital for lepers. There were several of these places on the various holy and saints routes in medieval Cornwall.

Back to the church of St. Nivet and follow Rectory Road south and then at Rectory Hill walk east through the tunnel under the A30, even in winter roaring with traffic.

At Reperry Cross you will find the charming old guide stone with a hand showing the way to Lanivet. *The only trouble is that the stonemason did not quite manage to get the whole word Lanivet onto the stone! The name may mean Petroc's Ford. The Celtic is* Re-perrec, re *meaning ford and* Perrec *the Breton word for Petroc.*

Left at the crossroads and on to St. Ingunger where there was once a holy well and a pilgrimage chapel and here is another Celtic cross. Follow the markers south to Fentonpits and yet another cross. At a fork go south-west to Trebell and then south-east to Trebell Green. Just after a sharp right turn in the road you arrive at Helman Tor Gate from where you will see the granite outcrop of Helman Tor itself. Sadly this last section of the Forth an Syns cannot follow the ancient way. The Saints' Way marker at Helman Tor gate shows you that there are decisions to be made about which route to follow next but for now it is worth climbing up to the Tor for the view and decide later on which way you want to go when you set out on the third section of the walk.

On the top of Helman Tor, at 680m the second highest point of the Saints' Way, you will find yourself out on moorland with gorse, broom and willows all around. To the north you can make out the memorial to Sir Walter Raleigh Gilbert, an obelisk standing above Bodmin. Southwards Roche Rock rears up dark and threatening with its hermitage and chapel of St. Michael (patron saint of heights or sailors) and away towards St. Austell you will see the china clay works with their spoil tips. And to add to your final pleasure there is a 10 ton logan stone for you to rock just below the summit. What more could you ask!

34. THE SAINTS' WAY PART 3
HELMAN TOR. CRIFT DOWNS. LANLIVERY. PELYNTOR. CASTLE. MILLTOWN.

Distance:	Medium 4¹/₂ miles / 7¹/₂ kms
Difficulty:	Easy
Maps:	(See Map P151) Landranger 200
Start:	Helman Tor, Map Ref. SX 062616.

It would be a good thing to come back up to Helman Tor just for the view. It changes every time you come here, even by the minute, with different light and the shadows of the clouds scudding across the Cornish landscape. Even in mist and rain it has a wild charm and a feeling of being at one with the elements.

Set off south-east down the track beside Breney Common. You come to a car park and after that there is a walled track. A footpath goes off west but keep on along the track which was without doubt one of the really ancient, probably prehistoric, trading routes between the north and south coast. A link with the dark Ages and medieval times. After a while you will reach a small road.

Go on south-east to the crossroads where there is a disused chapel. The road climbs slowly up to Lanlivery perched on the top of the hill. *Here there is another lovely 15th century church with a tall pinnacled tower. It is the second highest church tower in Cornwall, the highest being at Probus. In the early days of the last century and before, they painted one side of the tower white to act as a landmark and navigation aid to sailors away out at sea off Gribben Head. There is something of a muddle as to which saint the church is dedicated to. Maybe there was a saint called Livri for the village was once known as Lanlivri. But there is a holy well of St. Brevita near the church and this could have been the first dedication which still stands. However in the Middle Ages the church was rededicated to St. Manacus and St. Dunstan and to this day the feast day is held on St. Dunstan's Day, 19 May, even though it is the church of St. Brevita. St. Dunstan was Archbishop of Canterbury in the 10th century. In the tower there is a board with rhymes to help the bellringers get the changes right. On the board there are also five little men wearing strange hats who must have been the five bellringers. Now there are eight bells but the picture has not been updated since 1811 when the three extra bells were hung!*

In the village is the Churchtown Farm Field Studies Centre where they arrange holidays for handicapped children; a marvellous project.

The Old Crown Inn near the church will provide you will all the refreshment you may require before you set off again on the last leg of this section of the Saints' Way.

From the church go along the eastern side and walk down some stone steps which will take you past another meeting-house which has been well restored. Follow the lane eastwards. By a cottage called Pelyntor, where the road turns south, go through the gate between two buildings where you soon climb a stile into fields.

Go up a slight hill to the junction of the A390 and B3269 where you will find a tall Celtic cross. For a while you have to walk east (left) towards Lostwithiel along the busy main road but soon you come to some granite gateposts on the right. Follow the lane by the posts and then turn right up a hill to a farm before going south on a green lane. This will take you to a minor road at Castle. *There are some fine views on this section of the walk across rolling countryside.*

From the Castle walk south on the road and take the left fork and wander on down by woods to Milltown, a charming little collection of cottages. If you have time you can follow a little path through woods and under the railway to have a look at the upper tidal reaches of the River Fowey, but Milltown marks the end of this stage of the Saints' Way.

35. THE SAINTS' WAY PART 4
MILLTOWN. LANTYAN. ST. SAMPSON'S CHURCH. GOLANT. SAW MILLS CREEK. FOWEY.

Distance:	Medium 5$^{1}/_{2}$ miles/9kms
Difficulty:	Easy
Maps:	Landranger 200
Start:	Milltown, Map Ref. SX 104578.

Set off south from Milltown under the railway bridge and take the lane to the left which climbs uphill. *Below you can make out an ancient farm called Lantyan which legend has it was once the palace where King Mark of Cornwall, uncle of Tristan, lived with his wife Iseult. May I refer you to Walk 14 for most of the information about this section of the Saints' Way.*

Otherwise the following are the main directions for the walk, with a few extra details for when you reach Fowey.

After Milltown you follow the lane as described. You will get marvellous glimpses out over the countryside and the River Fowey below. You might just make out the church of St. Winnow beside the estuary. Soon you will be walking by Lantyan and Woodgate woods until you come to the bottom of the valley. Do not go down the turning to Wringford Farm but go over the stream and start to climb up the far side. This will take you to the Forth an Syns sign and you now follow that route to St. Sampson's Church. *Looking back you can see why they used Lanlivery Church as a landmark for sailors for it stands out way back to the north. You should also be able to see Helman Tor.*

On now to Golant down the road from the church. *Charles Stuart camped near here in 1644 before the Parliamentarian army surrendered.*

You come to Sawmills Creek by Colvithick Wood and climb up to Penventinue where you turn left and leave Walk 14 to walk on down the lane until you come to the main road and Fowey. *A settlement has been here since before 1162 when reference was made to it as being connected to Tywardreath Priory. The name of course is also the name of the river. It comes from Foath or Fawyth which means a beech tree and you can see many of those near the River Fowey.*

In Fowey you will find Love Lane and a packhorse lane that takes you to Readymoney Cove. (I couldn't resist putting those names in!) *On the Esplanade there the house where Sir Arthur Quiller-Couch lived. You will see the Bodinnick Ferry, an ancient crossing place that dates back to 1344. Then there is the fine 15th century church of St. Fimbarros with its 126ft tower with four pinnacles, each with a weather-vane.* This is where the Saints' Way ends. *Near the church is a lovely Tudor house, rebuilt in the 1840s, called Place where the Treffry family lived.*

As you might expect there are many fine pubs and restaurants where you can celebrate the completion of this long journey from Padstow to Fowey, from the church of St. Petroc to the church of St. Fimbarros. I hope you will have felt and discovered something of the history of Cornwall following in the footsteps of these early traders and holy men and women from the Dark Ages.

36. ST. MICHAEL'S WAY
LELANT, CARBIS BAY. KNILL'S MONUMENT. LONGSTONE DOWNS. BOWL ROCK. TRENCROM HILL. NINNESBRIDGE CHAPEL. LUDGVAN. MARAZION. ST. MICHAEL'S MOUNT.

Distance: Long 12 miles / 19½ kms or 12½ miles / 20½ kms
Difficulty: Easy

| Maps: | (See Map P151) Landranger 203 |
| Start: | The church of St. Uny, Lelant, Map Ref. SW 548377. |

The St. Michael's Way is a new long distance path developed by Cornwall County Council with the help of Brederth Sen Jago (the Cornish Pilgrims of St. James) and the Cornish Bureau for European Relations.

From the 9th century huge numbers of pilgrims trekked across Europe on their way to the Cathedral of St. James in Santiago de Compostela in north-west Spain. But by the 16th century the numbers undertaking the long and difficult journey had dwindled and some of the routes were lost or fell into disrepair and many fine and interesting buildings where the pilgrims prayed and stayed have vanished.

The St. Michael's Way is one of the Santiago de Compostela routes partly for the same reason that the Saints' Way was walked. Pilgrims from Ireland and Wales could arrive by boat in the comparatively sheltered anchorage and harbours of St. Ives Bay, in St. Ives itself or Hayle, and could then travel on foot across the narrow neck of land to St. Michael's Mount, a departure point for the pilgrims on the next stage of their journey to Spain. Like the Saints' Way this walk across land avoided the rocky cliffs and rough seas around Land's End.

Many little ships were licensed (licences even in those days) to carry pilgrims from Mount's Bay. St. Michael's Mount itself was a place where the pilgrims stopped to pray to the Archangel Michael for protection for their journey. It was here, of course, that the saint was seen in a vision by fishermen in AD 495. And also when they got to the Cathedral of Santiago de Compostela they would find that the shrine of St. Michael was immediately above that of the Apostle St. James, the patron saint of the Cathedral. St. Michael has always been associated with high places where he defeated evil, often depicted by a dragon lunging out of the swirling clouds.

Quite clearly this Way was an important link with the missionaries who brought Christianity to Cornwall, the pilgrims themselves, and with Cornish history. Work started in 1987 to define and re-establish the route across this part of Cornwall and to set up the walk; all part of a European initiative to open again the old pilgrims' routes to Santiago de Compostela.

The whole route is waymarked and signposted using the traditional pilgrim's symbol, a scallop shell, in a stylised form, which is the Council of Europe's sign for pilgrim routes. The arrows are painted in the colours specified by the Countryside Commission:

yellow for footpaths, blue for bridleways, and red for byways. Cornwall County Council uses black arrows on roads.

As the walk is so clearly waymarked and signed I shall not give directions as to which way to go, for the signs will tell you. However I shall give details of the interesting and unusual things to see en route, as well as legends and stories.

The start is at the church of St. Uny at Lelant. It was built in Norman times but in 1424 it was reconsecrated after extensive Gothic rebuilding. Some of the Norman arching remains as well as 15th century arches and a curious font and dial. It still stands quite close to the shifting sands and in the time of James I a hurricane almost destroyed the church and the sands almost covered it. In the 1720s it was restored and rebuilt only to be badly damaged once again by storms in 1872.

You will find yourself walking up a path called Wheal Margery Lane which is yet another reminder of the tin mining of Cornwall. *Wheal is the word used for a mine working and Wheal Margery was indeed an old tin mine that, records show, was working in the 1770s. It ran out under the seabed and they had a constant problem with sea water seeping in.*

The path takes you to Knill's Monument. *John Knill was one of the worthy local citizens and indeed mayor of St. Ives but born in Callington in 1733. His main job was that of Collector of Customs. He was also a man keen on improving the area, with roads, and the lives of the local people. He moved to London in 1782 after 20 years in St. Ives but before he left he built the monument you can see now. He also left money in a trust for celebrations for local people to be held every five years. The first one was in 1801 and John Knill was still alive to take part in the ceremonies.*

The trust still holds money to repair the monument when necessary, to give money to ten little girls, the daughters of seamen, fishermen or miners, and two widows. On the feast day of St. James the Apostle, 25 July, the groups walk up the hill to the monument with a fiddler in front and the children dancing. There were also other categories for gaining prizes: the man and wife who had raised the largest family, the most worthy and deserving wife under 36 years old, the best net-knitter, the best fish-packer, and two deserving fish-boys! And ever since 1801, every five years, the celebrations have taken place without ever missing one.

The views from here are magnificent, looking along the north coast of Cornwall, down to the estuary and the ancient and historic harbour of Hayle. You can make out St. Ives with the island and chapel of St. Nicholas and inland the moors and tors of central Penwith.

The Longstone you come to is another early menhir, probably from the Bronze Age, so prehistoric man was up here long before the pilgrims.

On Longstone Downs the Cavaliers under Sir Richard Grenville defeated a small group of Roundheads in 1645.

The next point of interest is Bowl Rock which is a large round granite boulder rolled here by a giant who was playing bowls with a friend. Stories of giants appear all over Cornwall such as at St. Agnes and Carn Marth. Apparently Trencrom Hill, where you will be going soon, was full of giants. One, the Giant of Nancledra, had a rather nasty habit of swallowing children whole! There is another splendid story told of how two giants used to share a hammer and would throw it across to each other when they wanted to hand it over. However when one of the giants threw the hammer, by mistake it hit the wife of the giant of St. Michael's Mount on the head and killed her. The two giants roared with grief causing horrendous storms at sea!

On Trencrom Hill, as you will realise when you reach it, there is a fine example of an Iron Age hill-fort. Every time I visit one of these forts I am amazed by the work and skill that was needed in constructing the ramparts and the choice of the outstanding defensive positions. Here there are walls built between outcrops of rock and inside the fort there are many hut circles and two wells. It probably dates from 4th century BC. The whole of Trencrom Hill was given to the National Trust in 1946 by the Tyringham family as a memorial to all the Cornish men and women who gave their lives in the two world wars.

This is also a region of piskies or 'spriggans'. Tales about piskies are found all over Cornwall. A nine-year-old boy disappeared from St. Allen for over three weeks only to be found asleep on a bed of ferns. When woken he told a story of being taken by the Little People to a palace of silver and gold and being fed on fairy food. There are many accounts of people being 'pisky-led' and getting lost in familiar country or being led over the moors in a wild dance. Cows were milked dry mysteriously in some areas while in others it was considered good luck to have a pisky in the house.

Often there are rumours of gold to be found in ancient mounds and tumuli either from prehistoric times or even left behind by the giants! A local miner came up to Trencrom Hill on a brilliant moonlit night and started to dig for gold. As he dug the moon disappeared behind black clouds and it became almost totally dark. A storm arose and the wind howled over the moorland. There were sudden brilliant and blinding flashes of lightning with booming cracks of thunder. In the vivid flashes of light the miner saw hundreds of piskies, or spriggans, creeping out of the rocks all around. He threw down his spade and ran blubbering blindly from the hill.

So avoid the giants and the piskies and take a look at the view from up here. Looking south, there is Mount's Bay with Mousehole, Newlyn and Penzance further west. Away to the south-east you can make out the Lizard.

John Wesley set out from Exeter on 29 August 1743 to bring his form of Christianity to Cornwall. He settled in St. Ives for a while and preached all round the county, returning many times. You will see countless Methodist chapels, some large, some small, throughout Cornwall, many still in use, others that have been converted into houses. Ninnes Bridge Chapel is one such.

After a long section through another delightful no man's land across fields and along paths, lanes and roads you come down to Ludgvan. *This village dates back to Norman times and the Domesday. As always there was probably a Celtic cell here but it was the Normans who built the church and there are medieval paintings on the walls. It is said that anybody baptized in the well of St. Ludgvan will never be hanged!*

Quite a number of famous people lived here or nearby. Dr. William Borlaze was a well-known antiquarian and naturalist and was rector at Ludgvan for 50 years from 1722 to 1772. Dr. Oliver, the man who invented Bath Oliver biscuits, was born here. Finally the family of Sir Humphrey Davy, whose statue you will find in Penzance and who invented the miners' safety lamp, lived at Varfell just to the south of Ludgvan.

There is a choice of routes now as you will see. One swings east towards Crowlas and down to Gwallon before arriving at Marazion. The other is longer and goes west via Gulval and then follows the Coastal Path back east to Marazion.

The first way takes you by Rospeath and Truthwall. *This was the only way around the Marazion marshes in ancient times. Legend has it that this was where the last wolf in Cornwall lived until he was killed by local farmers after devouring a child.*

The route by Gulval has strong links with the pilgrims as many may well have waited here to get news of ships that could take them on the next stage of their voyage. Gulval Well, which is no longer there, had curing properties like many other wells in Cornwall. It was also used as the means of finding out about lost or stolen cattle or goods and even the well-being of friends, depending on how the water in the well behaved.

Marazion means Little Market and indeed it was a well-known and busy centre for trading. The locals claim it to be the oldest town in Cornwall with a charter dating back to 1257 and Henry III. Very often the pilgrims would rest and sleep here in Marazion and then walk across to St. Michael's Mount when the tide was low to get their blessings and prayers answered.

St. Michael's Mount is a fascinating sight and well worth a visit either by the causeway or by boat. It is linked, of course, with Mont Saint Michel in Normandy when William the Conqueror's brother Robert de Mortain granted the Cornish mount to the Benedictines of the French abbey. In 1135 a priory was built on the summit.

Much earlier St. Michael's Mount was probably the port of Ictis that was known to the Greek geographer Diodorus when he wrote about tin-mining and trading with Gaul.

Then during the wars with France Henry V captured the mount and in 1424 granted the priory to the Abbey of Syon at Twickenham. The harbour and the cobbled causeway date from this time. Henry VIII took it over in 1535 during the Dissolution of the Monasteries and it was then that it became a defensive castle. The Royalists were here during the Civil War but it fell to the Parliamentarians and Colonel John St. Aubyn was put in charge. He bought the mount in 1659 and one of his ancestors, Lord St. Levan, is the present owner and still lives in the castle. He gave it to the National Trust in 1954 to bring us up to date.

So you will have followed the pilgrims' route and visited St. Michael's Mount to pray for protection from the Archangel. What about seeing if you can get a boat to take you across to Brittany so that you can continue the pilgrimage to the Cathedral of St. James in Santiago de Compostela?!

37. THE TINNERS' WAY
ST. JUST. CAPE CORNWALL. CARN KENIDJACK. TREGSEAL STONE CIRCLE. TOWEDNACK. ST. IVES

Distance: · Long 13 miles / 20³/₄ kms
Difficulty: Moderate
Maps: (See Map P151) Landranger 203;
Pathfinder SW 33/34

This is yet another marvellous Way that leads from St. Just to St. Ives. It uses ancient routes and tracks, some of which link back into prehistoric times. Where the Way runs over the high granite spine of this part of Cornwall it most certainly was an ancient way from prehistory when these early men moved from one area of Penwith to another using the high ground to avoid the densely wooded lowlands where dangers might lurk from neighbouring marauding tribes to wolves and bears.

It could well be that minerals were transported along this and other tracks in the area from the Bronze Age until the 19th century (a period of over 4000 years). There is also a network of routes across this toe of Cornwall linking the little fishing villages with the inland settlements and right across from one side to the other.

However in spite of the existence of a mass of ancient tracks and routes many archaeologists will not commit themselves to acknowledging that there was definitely a 'Tinners' Way' or Forth an Stenoryon as it is known in Cornish. At the moment a lot of the Way is still being defined and rights of access may not have been settled along all the route. However it is possible to follow an interesting series of tracks and there are waymarks for some of the route.

Starts: 1. St. Just. 2. Cape Cornwall. Map Ref. SW 350318.

Both starts have their advantages. The St. Just one takes you more directly to some extraordinary stones, while the Cape Cornwall one sets off along the Coastal Path and passes a Stone Age and later an Iron Age headland fort and some old mine engine houses before coming down to the stones.

You will probably find time to look around St. Just which is an interesting little town. One of its claims to fame is that it is the most westerly town in mainland England. It was, but sadly no longer is, a busy mining town during the great days of Cornish tin and copper mining last century. The grey granite houses with their gables and the old inns give a feeling of a once thriving mining industry. Apparently the miners and even now the true local Cornish people call their town St. Oost!

John Wesley was here, preaching first in small cottages and then later to huge gatherings in the open air, many of whom were miners. He travelled hundreds of miles on horseback and on one occasion he preached six sermons and rode over 50 miles in three days. On these journeys special accommodation was provided for him by local people and one of these resting places was at St. Just. There are two fine Methodist chapels here, as you might expect, one with a Doric facade. There is also a solidly built 15th century granite church with two interesting frescoes, one of our Saviour and the other of St. George and the Dragon.

In the centre of the town is the ancient Plain-an-Gwarry or 'Playing Place' which is a grass-covered amphitheatre about 126ft in diameter where medieval miracle or mystery plays were once performed.

It is a short walk out to Cape Cornwall from St. Just if you are going to use this start. It is yet another interesting and exciting headland now owned by the National Trust. It is the only headland that uses the word Cape in its name in the whole of England. The meaning of the word Cape is a headland where two oceans or channels meet. In early times Cape Cornwall was known as the ancient Land's End because it is here that the English Channel and St. George's Channel meet, hence Cape.

You will notice the distinctive mine stack on the summit of the Cape and to the west side the little boats and huts down in Priest's Cove. Nothing to do with priests but a corruption of Porth East meaning the cove of St. Just.

Just offshore you can make out the treacherous rocks of the Brisons where many a ship has come to grief. It was also said that the rocks were once used as an open-air prison.

The views are tremendous. On really clear days, after rain, you might just make out the low smudges of the Scillies. While nearer, the Longships lighthouse guards the rocks of Carn Bras. The lovely sandy sweep of Sennen and Whitesand Bay is just below you.

The headland was where the Iron Age people built a fort and there was even a defensive ditch and bank across the neck of the Cape. You will also see the small chapel known as St. Helen's Oratory built originally within a circular wall from much later.

Set off along the Coastal Path north-east above Porth Ledden Cove before you drop steeply down into a little valley with its stream plunging to the sea. Yet another Iron Age fortified headland is to be seen, Kenidjack Cliff Castle, and you may well want to walk across to look for the various ditches and ramparts that remain as part of an extensive system of defences. There are barrows and hut circles in the area, and moulds, ceremonial axe-heads and lumps of almost pure copper have been found. To bring you up to date there are the remains of an old rifle range nearby!

All around here and along the coast northwards is one of the most amazing areas of industrial archaeology in Britain. *The crowns of many mines are to be seen with the gaunt engine houses, many well preserved and restored, reminding us of this incredible era of Cornish and indeed British history. If you have time it is worth walking to have a look down on the engine house of the famous cliffside mine of Botallack. The shaft of this old mine ran down under the sea and on really stormy nights the miners, working the late shifts, could hear the sound of the boulders grinding, rumbling and rolling about on the seabed just a few feet above their heads.*

The Coastal Path will take you past two more engine houses. Just by the second one leave the main track and take a lane going off to your right between fields. Cross stiles and follow tracks to Truthwall and then along another rough track to Kenython. Here swing north through a gate and onto the moorland by Carn Kenidjack through wire fencing. You should now be able to link up with the route that starts in St. Just and goes to Tregseal Circle and the holed stones.

If you have chosen the St. Just start then set off from the church east through Venton East Square and then down a steep lane to the road. Find the footpath going off right by the new houses. This will take you into the Tregseal valley and you follow the road past Hailglower Farm and then by a narrow lane, that can be very wet, onto the moors.

Tregseal Stone Circle is to your right and dates from the Bronze Age. At one time there were probably three circles but only one remains. Like so many of these circles it was vandalised partly by digging a quarry and by the stones being knocked over or taken for building. Only 10 of 17 stones remained.

The next interesting site is the holed stones, again to your right. There are three large stones all with holes in them that clearly have been bashed out with a blunt instrument. There is a broken fourth stone lying nearby and a fifth that was broken but has been cemented together. A sixth can be found a little up the hill to the north-east but as this hole appears to have been drilled out it may not belong to the same period as the others. The holed stones have powers to heal and induce fertility, or so it was believed.

Up to your left are the gaunt rocks of Carn Kenidjack, known as the Hooting Carn because of the noise that the wind makes as it whistles over the rocks. I am sure that early man must have found the weird-shaped rocks a powerful place of magic, for all around are prehistoric relics and remains.

And of course the piskies are here, as is the Devil!

The actual Tinners' Way goes to the north of Carn Kenidjack but there are quite a number of tracks and bridleways in this area so you will probably want to wander around looking at the various points of interest, the last being the Boslow Stone. You reach it by going back to the main bridleway that you might have crossed on your way to Carn Kenidjack and following it to a narrow stony lane until you come to a cross-tracks. *The stone is to your right. It lies on the boundary of the parishes of St. Just and Sancreed. There is a cross carved on one side and what could be JAC-TVENA on the other. This might be 'Hic Jacit Vena' - 'Here lies Vena'.*

Go back to the farm track and walk on to the Trewellard and Pendeen Road in an area with the marvellous name of Woon Gumpus.

The most direct route of the Tinners' Way from the Boslow Stone crosses the road and then goes along an unsurfaced road to Trehyllys Farm and along a small road to the Men-an-Tol Studio. However the most interesting way is to turn left along the road and walk until you come to the junction where one road goes to Trewellard while the other goes to Pendeen. From the layby on your right you will see the waymarked track that leads to Chun Quoit. Please look at Walk 29 for details of this section of the walk.

When you reach the Morvah to Madron and Penzance Road turn right as in Walk 29 to the Men-an-Tol Studio and follow Walk 28 to Men-an-Tol, Men Scryfa and the Four Parish Stone.

When you reach the Four Parish Stone you can, if you wish, go down the Maidens Stone Circle and then cut back to the Tinners' Way but eventually you need to walk past the drive of Brook Cottage and on to Bodrifty Settlement, another of the Bronze Age or possibly Iron Age villages. *All around are small fields where they probably grew corn.*

From here you can again divert to have a look at Mulfra Quoit. *Details of these Cornish quoits are given with Walks 28 and 29 that take you to Lanyon and Chun Quoits. The sad thing about Mulfra is that the 5 ton capstone fell during a violent storm in 1752.*

If you follow the Tinners' Way from Bodrifty Settlement you will come to the Newmill to Treen Road at Grove Corner. If you go to Mulfra Quoit you walk north-east to the same road and then follow it to Grove Corner.

Take the road east to Higher Kerrowe. Do not swing up north to Zennor on the road but go ahead to where the parishes of Zennor, Towednack and Gulval meet at a crossing that is known as the Bishops Head and Foot. An ancient granite cross stood here once and at one time the land around here was held by the Bishops of Exeter whose diocese stretched down into Cornwall.

An unsurfaced road leads you onto Lady Downs where you have a choice to get to Towednack by a southern route via Embla and Skillywadden or a northern route via Embla Vean, Amalveor and Beagletodn.

Another quoit is off to the north from this section of the Way so once again if you have time you might like to walk up to Zennor Quoit, but you will have to return to Towednack to finish the walk down to St. Ives.

The little squat church at Towednack is worth a visit. It is probably 13th century while some of the north wall and nave are Norman. The dumpy little tower without any pinnacles, which is unusual in this part of Cornwall, was added in 1500. There is a splendid legend that tells how the Devil kept visiting the church during the building of the tower and every time it reached a certain height he knocked it down. In the end the stonemasons gave up in total exasperation so they finished the tower off at the height the Devil left it and never added pinnacles!

There are some interesting crosses. One in the south porch, that is used now as a bench, is in the shape of a cross that came from an axe-cult with a goddess priesthood from pagan Crete in 1500 BC.

From the church turn right on the Nancledra Road and then over a stile into fields past Chytodden and on to Bussow Farm. On to the road now to St. Ives and Hellesveor Chapel on your left and the junction with the Land's End Road. Turn into Chyandour Close, then past St. John's Church and the St. Ives Rugby Football Club and work your way down to Porthmeor Beach to end at St. Nicholas Chapel on The Island.

St. Ives, of course, is one of Cornwall's most famous tourist towns with its 'miles of golden sands', while the brilliant blues of the sea make you almost believe that you are on the edge of the Mediterranean. It has also one of the great surfing beaches of Great Britain.

But it is an ancient borough and port dating back almost to prehistory and there is still a labyrinth of narrow, crooked, dark, roughly paved streets, alleys, courts and stairways that show its ancient roots.

Its real fame came in the days of the pilchard fishing industry that continued until the beginning of this century. Thirty million pilchards were caught in an hour and landed at St. Ives in 1834. There is another famous catch recorded when in 1868 16$\frac{1}{2}$ million pilchards were caught in just one seine net. The pilchards were piled into presses to extract the blood and oil while the resulting mush was salted and packed into hogsheads to be exported to Mediterranean countries. The result of this industry was that the whole town reeked of fish while the oil and blood stained the narrow streets.

As well as pilchards, tin and copper ore were also exported, while coal was brought in to be landed in the harbour at Smeaton's Pier which was built by the famous architect of the Eddystone Light; those of you who have been to Plymouth will have seen Smeaton's Tower on the Hoe.

The maze of little streets behind the harbour was divided into 'Downalong' where the fishermen lived with their families and 'Upalong' where the miners lived. Great feuds would rage, particularly between the young men, and many a terrible fight would take place on the quay. Sadly no miners are left now and there is a much diminished fishing industry, while 'trips round the bay' for the tourists are the modern pilchards to be squeezed dry!

If you wander round keep an eye out for the names of the little alleys and courts. The Digey, Puddingbag Lane, Fish Street, Rope Walk; they all tell a tale. The pub called the Sloop is where you will find many of the local fishermen and artists. Wesley spent a lot of time here as well as at St. Just (both ends of the Tinners' Way) and streets like Teetotal Street and Salubrious Street mark his influence and that of Methodism.

The church is dedicated to St. Ia, a female missionary who, legend has it, sailed across from Ireland on an ivy leaf! There is a lovely barrel roof here and an exquisite sculpture by Barbara Hepworth of Our Lady and Child.

Turner visited St. Ives in the 1880s, and later Whistler and Sickert, and this was soon followed by many other artists. They were attracted by the wide skies and pure light of Cornwall and began to settle here using the old fish lofts as their studios and living in the little cottages where the fishermen and miners once lived. The same was happening on the other side of the toe of Cornwall at Newlyn where Stanhope Forbes started the Newlyn School. Ben Nicholson, Peter Lanyon and of course Barbara Hepworth and the potter Bernard Leach all settled here as well as many others. Today there are still a large number of artists here and galleries

169

galore.

St. Ives makes a fitting end to this walk that takes you into the solitude of the high moors with the magic of prehistoric man to the hustle and bustle of a busy tourist town with a lot to see and do.

38. THE CAMEL TRAIL
PADSTOW. WADEBRIDGE. BODMIN. DUNMERE. POLEY'S BRIDGE.

Distance: Long. 1. Padstow to Bodmin 11 miles/17^{1}/$_{2}$ kms
2. Padstow to Poley's Bridge 16 miles/26kms

Difficulty: Easy

Maps: (See Map P151) Landranger 200

Start: Padstow. There are car parks at Padstow, Wadebridge and Bodmin. There are also car parks at Dunmere, Hellandbridge, Shell Woods and Poley's Bridge. This means that you can start the walk at any of these places and walk whichever way you wish. The snag, as always, is that someone will have to come and fetch you at the far end or you will have to walk back.

Please refer to Walk 32 for the details for Padstow. The Way itself has been developed by Cornwall County Council along the old disused railway track from Padstow via Wadebridge to Bodmin. But another branch of the Way follows the River Camel from Dunmere, where the route divides, upstream to Poley's Bridge.

You should have no difficulty in following the walk along the old railway track and then upstream along the River Camel, and there are waymarks. The Way is also marked on the maps.

There is a short story written by Sir Arthur Quiller-Couch, who was known by the nom de plume *of 'Q', called* Cuckoo Valley Railway *which quite clearly was about this line from Bodmin to Wadebridge. Apparently the line was one of the first steam railways not only in Britain but the world and was opened in 1834. Its main use in those days was to carry sand inland from Wadebridge to be spread on the fields of local farms which were extremely acid. Coming back down the line, to be exported from Wadebridge, were china clay and granite. But travel by train for passengers was becoming increasingly popular and soon the line became well known for its excursions and day trips. In 1846 the London and South Western Railway bought the line and in 1899 it was extended to Padstow and started the era of holiday train traffic which continued until the line was finally closed by Beeching in 1967. It carried the Atlantic Coast Express, one of the famous railway journeys of Britain.*

The wildlife is one of the most marvellous features of the Camel Trail and where the Camel Estuary begins to close in there is a Bird Hide near Tregunna, opposite the Walmsley Wildfowl Sanctuary. Shelduck and curlews as well as other waterfowl thrive here such as herons and other duck and there are increasing numbers of egrets. On the river itself you may be lucky to see both trout and salmon in the upper reaches while in the estuary bass and mullet swim in on the tide. Dippers and kingfishers live on the Dunmere to Poley's Bridge section and even the shy otter is returning where humans do not go too often. Foxes, badgers, deer and of course the ubiquitous rabbit are all there if you go gently and carefully with your eyes open. Wild flowers line the banks and fill the woods with colour and wonder and with the mild climate of the estuary, snowdrops and violets are to be found during what most of us would call winter!

A Countryside Officer is responsible for the management and promotion of the Camel Trail and a lot of further information is available (see Useful Addresses). During the season there are a couple of cafes along the route, other than Wadebridge, where you can get refreshments. There are also some honesty boxes for you to contribute to the upkeep of maintaining the trail, which I hope you will enjoy.

Because the walking is level for much of the route and because there are quite a number of easy access points it is a fine walk for the not so able and young, while the very young can be pushed in their prams! It means that many people who perhaps cannot easily get into the depths of the countryside on more difficult paths have a chance to get into this lovely unspoilt Cornish landscape.

APPENDICES

GLOSSARY OF CORNISH PLACE-NAMES

Bos, bot, bod	Home	Hayl, hel, el, hale	Estuary
Bre, brea, bray	Hill	Hen	Old
Byghan, bean,		Hyr, ear, ir	Long
vean	Small	Kelly, kil, col	Wood
Car, caer, gear	Fort, camp	Lan, land	Church
Carn	Rock, stone	Lys, lis, liz, les	Court
Chy, che, jy, ty	House, cottage	Men, mayn, maen	Stone
Cos, got, cot, coat,		Meneth, mena	Hill
coad	A wood	Mur, mear, vear	Big, great, large
Du, dhu, threw	Black, dark	Nans, nant, nance	Valley
Dun, din	Hill-fort	Noweth, newth	New
Eglos	Church	Pen, pedn	Head, end
Fenten, fenton,		Pol	Pool
venton	Spring, well	Pons, pont	Bridge
Glas, glaze	Green, blue	Porth, port	Bay, harbour
Gun, goon, un,		Res, ret, red	Ford
woon	Down, heath	Ros, rose, roose	Heath, downs
Gwartha, wartha,		Ruth	Red
worth	Upper	Tre, trev	Farm, village
Gwyn, wyn, wen,		Treth, dreth,	
win, widden	White	dreath	Beach
Hal, hale	Moor, heath	Whel, wheal	Mine

A look at the walks and maps of Cornwall will reveal how the Cornish language crops up in so many of the placenames. Very often the names are a combination of two or more of the words given above. As you might expect, being a Celtic language, there are enormous similarities with Welsh and Breton.

USEFUL ADDRESSES AND TELEPHONE NUMBERS

AIRPORTS
Bodmin Airport, Cardingham. Tel (0120882) 463
British International Helicopters Penzance. Tel (01736) 63871
Newquay Airport. Tel (016373) 860551

BRITISH RAIL PASSENGER INFORMATION, PENZANCE.
   Tel (01736) 65831

CAMEL VALLEY COUNTRYSIDE SERVICE, 3/5 Barn Lane, Cornwall
   PL31 1LZ. Tel (01208) 78087

CORNWALL COUNTY COUNCIL COUNTRYSIDE RANGERS, Tehidy
   Country Park, Camborne, Cornwall TR13 0HA. Tel (01209) 714494

CORNISH COUNTRYSIDE ACCESS SECTION, County Highways
   Department, County Hall, Truro, Cornwall TR1 3BE.
   Tel (01872) 74282

CORNISH COUNTRYSIDE ACCESS SECTION, Transportation and
   Estates Department, Western Group Centre, Radnor Road, Scorrier,
   Redruth, Cornwall TR16 5EH. Tel (01209) 820611

CORNISH TOURIST BOARD, 59 Lemon Street, Truro, Cornwall
   TR1 2SY. Tel (01872) 74057

COUNTRYSIDE COMMISSION (South West Regional Office), Bridge
   House, Sion Place, Clifton, Bristol BS8 4AS. Tel (0117) 9739966

INSTITUTE OF CORNISH STUDIES, Trevenson House, Pool, Redruth,
   Cornwall TR15 3PL. Tel (01209) 712203

NATIONAL TRUST, Cornwall Regional Office, Lanhydrock, Bodmin,
   Cornwall PL30 4DE. Tel (01208) 74281

NATURE CONSERVANCY COUNCIL, Cornwall Office, Trelissick,
   Feock, Truro, Cornwall TR3 6QL. Tel (01872) 865261/865938

NORTH CORNWALL HERITAGE COAST SERVICE, Barn Lane,
   Bodmin, Cornwall PL31 1LZ. Tel (01208) 74121

RAMBLERS ASSOCIATION, 1/5 Wandsworth Road, London SW8 2LJ

ROYAL SOCIETY FOR THE PROTECTION OF BIRDS, The Lodge, Sandy, Bedfordshire SG19 2DL

WEATHER FORECASTS. Tel (0891) 500404

WEST COUNTRY TOURIST BOARD, 60 St. David's Hill, Exeter, Devon. Tel (01392) 76351

YOUTH HOSTELS ASSOCIATION, National Office, 8 St. Stephens Hill, St. Albans, Hertfordshire. Tel (01727) 855215

BIBLIOGRAPHY

Balchin, W.G.V. *The Cornish Landscape* (Hodder and Stoughton)
Barton, R.M. *Cornwall's Structure and Scenery* (Tor Mark Press)
Bere, R. *The Nature of Cornwall* (Barracuda)
Betjeman, J. *Betjeman's Cornwall* (Murray)
Carter, C. *Cornish Shipwrecks* (Pan Books)
Cooke, I. *The Tinners' Way* (Men-an-Tol Studio)
Gill, M. *The Saints' Way* (Crown Copyright)
Guthrie, D. *The Complete Guide to Cornish Pubs* (Half Pint Press)
Heritage Coast Service leaflets and booklets
Hoskins, W.G. *The Making of the English Landscape* (Pelican)
Kittridge, A. *Cornwall's Maritime Heritage* (Twelveheads Press)
National Trust Coast of Cornwall Series (16 leaflets)
Paton, J.A. *Flowers of the Cornish Coast* (Tor Mark Press)
Rowse, A.L. *A Cornish Anthology* (Macmillan)
Soulsby, I. *A History of Cornwall* (Phillimore)
Stanier, P.H. *Cornwall's Mining Heritage* (Twelveheads Press)